D1630309

So you really want to learn

English

Book Three

Susan Elkin

Series Editor: Nicholas Oulton M.A. (Oxon.)

Independent Schools
Examinations Board

www.galorepark.co.uk

GALORE PARK

Published by ISEB Publications, an imprint of Galore Park Publishing Ltd
19/21 Sayers Lane, Tenterden, Kent TN30 6BW

www.galorepark.co.uk

Text copyright © Susan Elkin 2006
Illustrations copyright © Galore Park 2006

Typography by Typetechnique, London W1
Illustrations by Ian Douglass

Printed by Replika Press Pvt. Ltd., India

ISBN: 978 1 902984 92 6

First published 2006, reprinted 2007, 2009, 2011

Accompanying this course:
English Book 3 Answer Book   ISBN-13: 978 1 90298 93 3

Details of other Galore Park publications are available at
www.galorepark.co.uk

ISEB Revision Guides, publications and examination papers may also be obtained
from Galore Park.

Acknowledgements

As always, I have to thank Nicholas Oulton and Galore Park Publishing for acting as collective midwife to this book.

Thanks are also due to my husband Nicholas Elkin, who scrupulously reads everything I write before anyone else sees it and is the best critic anyone could have.

I should also like to thank Geraldine Matthews of Heath Mount School and Nigel Ramage of Papplewick School for their constructive comments and willingness to trial materials and provide feedback in the early stages.

The publishers are grateful for permission to use extracts as follows:

Chapter 1:   Extract from *Rebecca* by Daphne du Maurier reproduced with permission of Curtis Brown Group Ltd, London on behalf of the Estate of Daphne du Maurier 1938.

Chapter 2:   Extract from *The Grapes of Wrath* by John Steinbeck (Penguin Books, 2001) Copyright 1939 John Steinbeck.

Chapter 3:   'November' by Ted Hughes from *Poets of Our Time* by permission of Faber and Faber Ltd. 'November's weather' from the Royal Horticultural Society website by kind permission of the RHS.

Chapter 4:   'Lost Portrait of Mozart' article by Bojan Pancevski by kind permission of the Telegraph Group Ltd.

Chapter 5:   'The Wild Swans at Coole' by W B Yeats by kind permission of A P Watt Ltd on behalf of Michael B Yeats.

Chapter 6:   Extract from Oxford University website by kind permission of the University of Oxford. Extract from *Grasshopper* by Barbara Vine (Ruth Rendell) (Viking, 2000), Kingsmarkham Enterprises Ltd, 2000.

Chapter 7:   Extract from *Turbulence* by Jan Mark reproduced by permission of Hodder and Stoughton Limited. Extract from *Clinging to the Wreckage* by John Mortimer by kind permission of the author and Weidenfield & Nicholson, an imprint of The Orion Publishing Group.

Chapter 8:   Extract from *Animal Farm* by George Orwell (Copyright © George Orwell, 1945) by permission of Bill Hamilton as the Literary Executor of the Estate of the Late Sonia Bronwell Orwell and Secker & Warburg Ltd.

Chapter 9:   Extract from *Birdsong* by Sebastian Faulks, published by Hutchinson/Vintage. Reprinted by permission of The Random House Group Ltd.

Chapter 10: 'Getting married this year?' article by David Sapsted by kind permission of the Telegraph Group Ltd.

Photo credits

The publishers are grateful to these organisations for the following images:

Chapter 1:   Easter Island: John Mead/Science Photo Library
La Belle Dame Sans Merci, Exhibition 1902 (oil on canvas) by Sir Frank Dicksee (1853-1928) © Bristol City Museum and Art Gallery, UK/The Bridgeman Art Library

Chapter 2:   Goblin Market: Mary Evans Picture Library
Waters Motor Co. Used Car Lot, photographer Angus B McVicar, 1903-1964 © Robertstock

Chapter 4:   Wolfgang Amadeus Mozart: bpk/Gemäldegalerie, SMB/Foto Jörg. P. Anders

Chapter 5:   Cleopatra in her barge on the Nile: Mary Evans Picture Library

Chapter 7:   The Past and Present, 1860 (oil on canvas) by William McTaggart (1835-1910) Private Collection/ © Bourne Fine Art, Edinburgh, Scotland/The Bridgeman Art Library

Chapter 9:   Imperial War Museum Neg no CO2533

Contents

Chapter 9

Chapter 10

Literary terms

Introduction for pupils

Reading matters

Welcome to *So You Really Want to Learn English Book 3*. If you have worked your way through Books 1 and 2 you will recognise the format. A newcomer to the series? Then I hope you enjoy the mixture of fiction, poetry, non-fiction and various sorts of language activity that each chapter offers.

I also hope that the recommendations in 'Have you read?' will lead you to some books which you might not otherwise read – and that you find them as engrossing as I do.

There are many good reasons for being a 'bookaholic' (that's a neologism, by the way). The first, of course, is that it's a great pleasure to bury yourself in a really gripping, interesting book. Another reason is that reading is a fine way of learning vocabulary, grammar and style. And any teacher will tell you that the more you read the better you will write. Bookish people tend to be very knowledgeable too because they are always effortlessly soaking up bits of information from their reading.

One of the important things to understand about English is that there are very few right and wrong answers. It's very different from, for example, maths. When you read a passage or poem you are quite likely to notice something new that teachers, pupils or the author of this book have not noticed before. Or you might read it in a different way so that your understanding is not the same as other people's. That can lead to very interesting discussions and is one of the great joys of studying English.

Remember, too, that you are probably reading some of these passages and poems for the first time. Several – Keats's 'La Belle Dame Sans Merci' (page 7) and the extract from *Mansfield Park* (page 110), for example, are very famous. You will almost certainly return to them and re-read them occasionally for the rest of your life – and, because you're an alert and thoughtful person, you will go on noticing new things. So don't expect to understand everything there is in a text when you first read it at school! The work you do there is the beginning of your journey of discovery, not the end.

Each chapter contains a section called 'Functions of language'. This is new for Book 3. It is an introduction to some of the many ways in which writers use language for a whole range of different purposes. I think you will find this an interesting aspect of English to study.

So – go on enjoying your work on this wonderful language of ours and the astonishing variety of fascinating texts which have been written in it.

Happy travelling!

Susan Elkin, September 2007

Introduction for teachers

So you really want to learn English Book 3 is intended for pupils in Year 8 and meets the requirements of the new ISEB syllabus affecting papers from 2008 onwards. There is also extension into off-piste learning and development – especially through wider reading.

Every comprehension activity – three in each chapter – leads pupils to use the text as evidence for their answers: fiction, non-fiction or poetry.

The emphasis on reading offers plenty of opportunity for each pupil to develop his or her ability to read with discrimination and to express a response to reading. Most of the rotating themes for Common Entrance are visited in, and threaded through, the chapters.

Some of the chosen extracts are deliberately very challenging. Every teacher will have his or her own way of helping Key Stage 3 pupils to meet that challenge at an appropriate level and there are plenty of my thoughts and responses in the parallel Answer Book. And perhaps every teacher would do well to put, writ large, on the classroom wall T S Eliot's famous maxim: 'Poetry can communicate before it is understood.' No English teacher should expect pupils to understand, on first acquaintance, everything there is to understand about some of the finest writing in English. They are, after all, at the very beginning of a life-long learning adventure.

Users of this book will soon be progressing to GCSE – hence the introduction to topics like First World War literature and the multifarious functions of language which they will need in Years 10 and 11.

Susan Elkin, September 2007

Chapter 1

Mysteries past

The narrator of Daphne du Maurier's famous 1938 novel **Rebecca** *is curious about Rebecca, her husband's dead first wife. One day she explores an unfamiliar part of the house and discovers the mysterious Rebecca's bedroom.*

1   I turned the handle of the door and went inside. It was dark, of course, because of the shutters. I felt for the electric light switch on the wall and turned it on. I was standing in a little ante-room, a dressing room, I judged, with big wardrobes round the wall, and at the end of the room was another door, open, leading to a larger room. I went through to

5   this room and turned on the light. My first impression was one of shock because the room was furnished as though in use.

I had expected to see chairs and tables, swathed in dustsheets, and dustsheets too over the great double bed against the wall. Nothing was covered up. There were brushes and combs on the dressing table, scent and powder. The bed was made up. I saw the gleam of

10   white linen on the pillowcase and the tip of a blanket beneath the quilted coverlet. There were flowers on the dressing table, and on the table beside the bed. Flowers too on the mantelpiece. A satin dressing gown lay on a chair and a pair of bedroom slippers beneath. For one desperate moment I thought that something had happened to my brain, that I was seeing back into time and looking upon the room as it used to be, before she died. . . In a

15   minute Rebecca herself would come back into the room, sit down before the looking glass at her dressing table, humming a tune, reach for her comb and run it through her hair. If she sat there I should see her reflection in the glass and she would see me too, standing like this by the door. Nothing happened. I went on standing there, waiting for something to happen. It was the clock ticking on the wall that brought me to reality again. The hands

20   stood at twenty-five past four. My watch said the same. There was something sane and comforting about the ticking of the clock. It reminded me of the present, and that tea would soon be ready for me on the lawn. I walked slowly into the middle of the room. No, it was not used. It was not lived in any more. Even the flowers could not destroy the musty smell. The curtains were drawn and the shutters closed. Rebecca would never come

25   back to the room again. Even if Mrs Danvers did put the flowers on the mantelpiece and the sheets on the bed, they would not bring her back. She had been dead now for a year. She lay buried in the crypt of the church with all the other dead de Winters.

I could hear the sound of the sea very plainly. I went to the window and swung back the shutter. The long shaft of light made the electric light look false and yellow. I opened

30   the shutter a little more. The daylight cast a white beam upon the bed. It shone upon the nightdress case lying on the pillow. It shone on the glass top of the dressing table, on the brushes and on the scent bottles.

35 I realised for the first time since I had come into the room that my legs were trembling, weak as straw. I sat down on the stool by the dressing table. My heart no longer beat in a strange excited way. It felt as heavy as lead. I looked about me in the room with a sort of dumb stupidity. Yes, it was a beautiful room. Mrs Danvers had not exaggerated that first evening. It was the most beautiful room in the house. That exquisite mantelpiece, the ceiling, the carved bedstead and the curtain hangings, even the clock upon the wall and the candlesticks upon the dressing table beside me, all were things I would have

40 loved and almost worshipped had they been mine. They were not mine though. They belonged to someone else. I put out my hand and touched the brushes. One was more worn than its fellow. I understood it well. There was always one brush that had the greater use. Often you forgot to use the other, and when they were taken to be washed, there was one that was still quite clean and untouched. How white and thin my face

45 looked in the glass, my hair hanging lank and straight. Did I always look like this? Surely I had more colour as a rule? The reflection stared back at me, sallow and plain.

I got up from the chair and went and touched the dressing gown on the chair. I picked up the slippers and held them in my hand. I was aware of a growing sense of horror, of horror turning to despair. I touched the quilt on the bed, traced with my fingers the

50 monogram on the nightdress case, R de W, interwoven and interlaced. The letters were corded and strong against the golden satin material. The nightdress was in the case, thin as gossamer, apricot in colour. I touched it, drew it out from the case, put it against my face. It was cold, quite cold. But there was a dim mustiness about it still where the scent had been. The scent of white azaleas. I folded it, and put it back into the case and as I

55 did so, noticed with a sick, dull aching in my heart that there were creases in the night-dress. The texture was ruffled. It had not been touched since it was last worn.

(Slightly abridged from *Rebecca* by Daphne du Maurier, 1938)

Exercise 1.1

Read the extract from *Rebecca* and answer the following questions:

1. Who do you think Mrs Danvers is?

2. Give another word for (a) swathed (line 7), (b) sallow (line 46) and (c) monogram (line 50).

3. What is the narrator's married name?

4. Write a paragraph summarising what you learn about the narrator from this passage.

5. In what ways does Rebecca seem to have been different from the narrator?

6. What horrifies the narrator about Rebecca's nightdress and why?

Mystery of Easter Island

1   Easter Island, just fifteen miles long and ten miles wide, has 887 stone statues. Each weighs several tons and some are more than nine metres tall. But nobody knows why or how they got there so they qualify as one of the world's great mysteries.

5   Easter Island, which belongs to Chile, is in the southern Pacific Ocean and is one of the remotest spots on the globe. It lies 2,300 miles west of the coast of Chile and 2,500 miles southeast of Tahiti. The closest island is 1,400 miles away.

Imagine Easter Day, 1772, when a Dutch captain landed there. He was the first European to set foot on the island which at that time was virtually uninhabited. He and his crew were stunned by that, now famous, line of towering statues.

10   Scientists and others have tried ever since that first landing to solve the mystery of the statues. This is one theory:

Easter Island was inhabited by Polynesian seafarers who arrived in about 400 A.D. They had travelled thousands of miles in their canoes, guided by the stars, sun, ocean rhythms, sky colour, cloud formation, wave patterns and bird flight paths. For some

15   reason they stayed.

This would tally with Thor Heyerdahl's work. A Norwegian explorer and scientist, Heyerdahl believed that the Polynesians sailed across the ocean in small craft. In 1947, with five other men, he proved it was possible by building a traditional balsa wood raft and crossing the Pacific on it. The voyage took 101 days.

20   There seem to have been two classes of races of Easter Island inhabitant: those with long ears and those with short ears. The long-eared people were the rulers. The short-eared, who came earlier, were the workers. That is why, according to one theory, most of the statues have long ears.

Not all the statues on the island stand upright or in line. Perhaps only a few made it to
25   their intended destination while the rest were abandoned along the way.

The statues were carved out of the top edge of the walls of an inland volcano on the island. Once a statue was carved, it was rolled or dragged down to the base of the volcano. Then it was raised by leverage and ropes tied around it.

The island's ancient grass, which has now almost disappeared because of over-grazing by
30   herded sheep, was tough and could have been made into strong ropes. The theory is that the ropes were wrapped around the statue, which then functioned as a pulley. Two groups of men would pull first from one side and then the other so that the statue inched forward.

It would have taken many laborious months, but a statue could have been 'walked' down to the ocean in this way. Each one which made it was placed in a line. They face
35   away from the sea towards the centre of the island.

Some scientists think that if a statue fell over in transit, as often must have happened, there was no way of lifting it again. So they simply returned to base and carved another one. That would explain why there are statues scattered about the island, not erected and apparently at random.

40   The sculpting and movement of these statues required the co-operation of the entire population of the island. So presumably there was a powerful religious motive. The people must have believed with deep conviction that they were required by their gods to undertake this extraordinary work.

At its peak, the population of Easter Island may have been as high as 11,000. When the
45   first Europeans finally arrived on the island, most of these people had died out.

Interestingly, ancient Easter Islanders could write and had their own unique system. No other Pacific Islanders knew how to write. Neither did American Indians.

Their diet poses unanswered questions too. Easter Islanders lived on sweet potatoes, which they farmed. Sweet potatoes originated in the Americas. How did the Easter
50   Islanders get them? It is hardly likely that a few adventurous Easter Islanders rowed or sailed 2,300 miles to Chile and returned with these vegetables.

Could Easter Island have been colonised by people from Chile? Probably not. DNA samples from graves on Easter Island have shown that these people were Polynesians, not American Indians. But Heyerdahl argued that the ancient Polynesians cremated their
55   dead which destroys DNA. He thought that the graves found on Easter Island in modern times belonged to a later influx of Polynesians.

(Researched and written by Susan Elkin, 2006)

Exercise 1.2

Read the extract *Easter Island* and answer the following questions:

1.   Explain in your own words why the Easter Island statues 'qualify as one of the world's great mysteries'.

2.   Give another word or phrase for (a) ocean rhythms (line 13), (b) leverage (line 28) and (c) colonised (line 52).

3.   What is puzzling about the diet of the ancient Easter Islanders?

4.   Why, according to one theory, do most of the statues have long ears?

5.   What prompted Thor Heyerdahl to cross the Pacific Ocean on a raft?

6.   Why do those who study Easter Island presume that the statues are religious in origin?

7.   In a short paragraph summarise how the statues might have been moved down to the sea from the spot where they were carved.

8.   What is the problem with Easter Island DNA evidence?

La Belle Dame Sans Merci

1   O what can ail thee, knight-at-arms,
        Alone and palely loitering?
   The sedge has withered from the lake,
        And no birds sing.

5   O what can ail thee, knight-at-arms,
        So haggard and so woe-begone?
   The squirrel's granary is full,
        And the harvest's done.

   I see a lily on thy brow
10   With anguish moist and fever dew;
   And on thy cheeks a fading rose
        Fast withereth too.

I met a lady in the meads,
    Full beautiful – a faery's child,
15   Her hair was long, her foot was light,
    And her eyes were wild.

I made a garland for her head,
    And bracelets too, and fragrant zone;
She looked at me as she did love,
20   And made sweet moan.

I set her on my pacing steed
    And nothing else saw all day long,
For sideways would she lean, and sing
    A faery's song.

25   She found me roots of relish sweet,
    And honey wild and manna dew,
And sure in language strange she said,
    'I love thee true.'

She took me to her elfin grot,
30   And there she wept and sighed full sore;
And there I shut her wild, wild eyes
    With kisses four.

And there she lullèd me asleep,
    And there I dreamed – Ah! Woe betide!
35   The latest dream I ever dreamed
    On the cold hill's side.

I saw pale kings and princes too,
    Pale warriors, death-pale were they all;
They cried – 'La Belle Dame Sans Merci
40   Hath thee in thrall!'

I saw their starved lips in the gloam
    With horrid warning gapèd wide,
And I awoke and found me here,
    On the cold hill's side.

45   And this is why I sojourn here
    Alone and palely loitering,
Though the sedge is withered from the lake,
    And no birds sing.

(John Keats, 1819)

Exercise 1.3

Read the poem 'La Belle Dame Sans Merci' and answer the following questions:

1. Who narrates the first three verses or stanzas of the poem? Who speaks the rest of the poem?

2. Explain in your own words why the knight-at-arms is 'alone and palely loitering' (line 46).

3. What is the mood of the knight-at-arms?

4. How does Keats make the surroundings reflect the mood of the knight-at-arms?

5. Explain the meaning of (a) ails (lines 1 and 5), (b) steed (line 21), (c) thrall (line 40) and (d) sojourn (line 45).

6. Choose and comment on three words or phrases which interest you in this poem.

Exercise 1.4

Your turn to write:

1. Write an imaginary or factual account of visiting a mysterious place.

2. Using the passage above – and further information gained from elsewhere if you wish – write an advertisement for Easter Island suitable for a Sunday newspaper or travel brochure.

3. Imagine you are La Belle Dame Sans Merci. Describe your encounter with the knight-at-arms. You could write this as a prose story or you could make it a poem, perhaps using the same stanza shape as Keats.

4. Research and write an article about a real-life, unsolved mystery such as the finding of the Marie Celeste, the possibility that there was a female pope in disguise in the ninth century or what happened to the infant princes who died in the Tower of London in 1483. And there are many others. Get your information from books and/or the internet.

5. Continue the story which begins in the extract from *Rebecca*.

6. Write in any way you wish about mystery.

Grammar and punctuation

Sentences

Remember that a sentence is a self-contained unit of communication. Think of it as a box with its capital letter at the beginning and full stop (which may be an exclamation or question mark) at the end.

Inside the box quite a lot can happen.

> Some scientists think that if a statue fell over in transit, as often must have happened, there was no way of lifting it again.

Here the main sentence, with two main verbs, is 'Some scientists **think** that if a statue fell over in transit there **was** no way of lifting it again'. The clause 'as often must have happened' is an extra so it is marked off with a pair of commas within the main 'box'.

> In a minute Rebecca herself would come back into the room, sit down before the looking glass at her dressing table, humming a tune, reach for her comb and run it through her hair.

Within this sentence Daphne du Maurier has linked five statements in a list, separated by commas. Rebecca would 1. come back, 2. sit down, 3. be humming, 4. reach and 5. run. Each of these statements has a main verb (known as a finite verb) except 'humming a tune' which is a participle, part of a verb doing the work of an adjective.

When you construct sentences make sure you build a secure box. Then you can use other punctuation inside it if you need to.

That way you will never fall into the very common and lazy mistake of ending sentences with commas.

Exercise 1.5

Punctuate these six sentences. Put in the capital letter and full stop first so that your outer 'box' is secure:

1. although he was frightened because he did not understand what was happening james opened the door firmly but quietly

2. did you really shout to frighten off any possible intruder as you entered the house switched on the lights and noticed that something seemed to be wrong

3. sit up shut up listen and take plenty of notes

4. in his novel bleak house charles dickens creates a character mr krook who dies through spontaneous combustion an unexplained phenomenon which has long fascinated human beings

5. all over the world there are statues in catholic churches and cathedrals usually of the virgin mary which people say they have seen weeping real physical tears sometimes of blood

6. daphne du mauriers best known novel dates from 1938 and although she wrote many others as well as some short stories and biographies nothing ever touched the popularity of rebecca except possibly my cousin rachel which was published in 1951

Changing fashions

Hyphens are **obsolescent.** That means that they are gradually disappearing from use. If they ever disappear completely they will be **obsolete**.

Today they are rarely used to link nouns or nouns and adjectives to make a different compound word. Generally we no longer hyphenate walking stick (walking-stick), ice cream (ice-cream) or sea cow (sea-cow). We use far fewer hyphens than we once did, although we still use them in words like sister-in-law.

Nearly two centuries ago when Keats wrote La Belle Dame Sans Merci hyphens were usual in, for example, a compound like 'death-pale'. Even 70 years ago when *Rebecca* was written hyphens were routinely used in words like 'night-dress' and 'dressing-table'.

Hyphens are still used occasionally by typesetters who have to break a word (between syllables) at the end of a line but most will try to avoid this clumsiness.

On the whole there is a trend today to use less punctuation rather than more so that a page of writing looks 'cleaner'.

Punctuation, like almost everything else, is affected by fashion. For another example, notice Daphne du Maurier's long paragraphs. Most 21st century writers would use shorter ones.

Spelling and vocabulary

The narrator of *Rebecca* passes though an **ante-room**.

ante is the Latin word for 'before' or 'in front'. Notice that it is spelled with an 'e'. The room was like a hallway which led into another room.

anti is the Latin word for 'against'. So an antiseptic is a chemical which works against infection and an antitank missile is one which is fired at tanks and heavy machinery in war. Notice that it is spelled with an 'i'.

Exercise 1.6

Provide words to fit these definitions. Be careful to spell them correctly with an 'i' or an 'e':

1. Describes a device such as a burglar alarm, lock or intruder light.

2. Something which is third before the end in a list.

3. Describes events before the biblical story of Noah's Flood.

4. To foresee or act before something happens.

5. Before birth.

6. Body of moving air of higher pressure than surrounding air so that pressure decreases from the centre.

Plurals

Some people have difficulty forming the plural of words that end in '-y'. It is actually quite simple. If the preceding letter is a **vowel** then the plural is usually formed by adding 's'. Thus:

to**y**	to**ys**
donke**y**	donke**ys**
affra**y**	affra**ys**

But if the 'y' is preceded by a **consonant**, we change the 'y' to an 'i' and add 'es'. Thus:

ovar**y**	ovar**ies**
abilit**y**	abilit**ies**
popp**y**	popp**ies**
rub**y**	rub**ies**

Exercise 1.7

What is the plural of these words?

1. reliquary
2. decoy
3. plutocracy

4. refectory
5. tercentenary
6. foray

Now write a sentence for each word to show you understand the meaning of each of these words. You may use either the singular or the plural form. A dictionary will help you.

Note:

Like punctuation, spelling sometimes changes with time. Notice Keats's spelling of fairy as 'faery'. Actually by 1819, 'fairy' would have been usual. Keats is using an old spelling because in 'La Belle Dame Sans Merci' he wants to create a poem with a timeless, romantic atmosphere. This will be explored in the next section.

Functions of language

Creating atmosphere

The atmosphere in the passage from *Rebecca* is sinister and full of suspense. Daphne du Maurier achieves this by

● using a lot of detail to keep the reader waiting and to show us how the narrator is feeling

● using a slow pace – the incidents probably take longer to tell than they would to happen so the effect is like a slow motion film

- using 'jerky grammar' including some sentence fragments instead of conventionally correct sentences ('Flowers too on the mantelpiece.' 'The scent of white azaleas.')
- short, very direct sentences interspersed with long ones ('The bed was made up.' 'Nothing happened.' 'The texture was ruffled.')
- phrases breathlessly tucked into the ends of long sentences ('scent and powder', 'weak as straw', 'sallow and plain')
- emphasising sounds, especially the ticking clock
- including smells such as the azaleas and the unwashed nightdress

Keats creates an atmosphere of mournful longing and sadness in 'La Belle Dame Sans Merci' by

- repetition of soft consonants like 'l' and 's' ('alone and palely loitering'), a technique known as **consonance**
- using long, slow sounds which sound like cries of pain ('made sweet moan', 'woe betide')
- choosing old forms of words such as 'withereth' instead of 'withers', 'hath' for 'has' and 'thee' for 'you'
- using four line stanzas which end with an abrupt, short, fourth line. Most of these contain only single syllable words which fall like hammer blows and sound very heavy and unhappy. ('no birds sing', 'On the cold hill's side')
- including words with negative associations – 'withered', 'woe-begone', 'ail'

Exercise 1.8

Write either a two stanza poem or two paragraphs of prose. Take as your subject either someone who is frightened or someone who is deeply unhappy. Use some of the techniques detailed above to make your writing atmospheric.

Speaking and listening

1. Prepare a reading aloud of any of the three passages in this chapter. Work out how to get the best out of the passage you choose. Perform it to the class or a small group. You might also record your work.

2. Work in a small group. Devise a ghost story that you can tell as a group. Then share your work with another group.

3. Work with a partner. Discuss 'La Belle Dame Sans Merci' in detail. Do you think the poem is effective and, if so, why?

4. Work with a partner. One of you is the narrator of *Rebecca*. The other is her husband, Maxim, when she tells him about her visit to his late wife's bedroom. Work out your conversation.

Have you read?

These books, stories and poems are either by the authors of the extracts in this chapter or they are about mysteries:

Rebecca by Daphne du Maurier (1938) Virago
My Cousin Rachel by Daphne du Maurier (1951) Virago
Daphne du Maurier by Margaret Forster (1993) Arrow
The Woman in Black by Susan Hill (1983) Vintage
'The Eve of St Agnes' by John Keats (This is can be found in many anthologies and most
    selections of Keats's verse)
The Kon-tiki Expedition by Thor Heyerdahl (1948) Flamingo
The Mammoth Encyclopaedia of the Unsolved by Colin Wilson (2000) Mammoth
The Oxford Book of Victorian Ghost Stories edited by Michael Cox and R A Gilbert
    (2003) OUP
Fingersmith by Sarah Waters (2003) Virago *
The Woman in White by Wilkie Collins (1860) Penguin Summer Classics *

* Recommended for very keen readers and for scholars

And if you've done all that

- Read *Rebecca* (if you haven't already done so). Then read *Jane Eyre* by Charlotte Brontë (1848). Most critics are convinced that Daphne du Maurier was very much influenced by *Jane Eyre*. Work out why and decide how far you agree.

- Watch the 1940 film of *Rebecca*, directed by Alfred Hitchcock and starring Laurence Olivier as Maxim de Winter. It is now regarded as a cinema classic and will be in almost any DVD or video library. View it very critically. Decide why it was, and is, judged as a great film. Or, if you disagree, work out your reasons.

- Research the life of John Keats who died when he was only 26. Prepare an informative wall poster for the classroom about him.

Chapter 2

Selling something?

Desperately poor farm workers in the state of Oklahoma in the 1930s are migrating in their thousands to California where they think they will be better off. So they sell most of their possessions to buy a lorry, known as a 'car', to travel in.

1   In the towns, on the edges of the towns, in fields, in vacant lots, the used-car yards, the wreckers' yards, the garages with blazoned signs – Used Cars, Good Used Cars. Cheap transportation, three trailers. '27 Ford, clean, Checked cars, Guaranteed Cars. Free radio. Car with 100 gallons of petrol free. Come in and look. Used Cars. No overhead.

5   A lot and a house large enough for a desk and a chair and a blue book. Sheaf of contracts, dog-eared, held with paper clips, and a neat pile of unused contracts. Pen – keep it full, keep it working. A sale's been lost 'cause a pen didn't work.

Those sons-of-bitches over there ain't buying anything. Every yard gets 'em. They're lookers. Spend all their time looking. Don't want to buy no cars; take up your time.

10   Owners with rolled-up sleeves, salesmen, neat deadly, small intent eyes watching for weaknesses.

Watch the woman's face. If the woman likes it we can screw the old man. Start 'em on that Cad. Then you can work them down to that '26 Buick. 'F you start on the Buick, they'll go for a Ford.

15   What you want is transportation, ain't it? No baloney for you. Sure the upholstery is shot. Seat cushions ain't turning no wheels over.

Like to see that one? Sure, no trouble. I'll pull her out of the line.

Get 'em under obligation. Make 'em take up your time. Don't let 'em forget they're taking up your time. People are nice, mostly. They hate to put you out. Make 'em put

20   you out, an' then sock it to them.

Yes sir, '22 Dodge. Best goddamned car Dodge ever made. Never wear out. Low compression.

Flags, red and white, white and blue – all along the kerb. Used Cars. Good Used Cars.

Today's bargain – up on the platform. Never sell it. Makes folks come in, though. If we

25   sold that bargain at that price we'd hardly make a dime. Tell 'em it's just sold. Take out that yard battery before you make delivery. Put in that dumb cell. Christ, what they want for six bits. Roll up your sleeves – pitch in. This ain't gonna last. If I had enough jalopies I'd retire in six months.

30 Listen Jim, I heard that Chevy's rear end. Sounds like bustin' bottles. Squirt in a couple of quarts of sawdust. Put in some gears too. We got to move that lemon for thirty-five dollars. Bastard cheated me on that one. I offer ten an' he jerks me to fifteen, an' then the son-of-a-bitch took the tools out.

35 Piles of rusty ruins against the fences, rows of wrecks in black, fenders, grease-black wrecks, blocks lying on the ground and a pig-weed growing up through the cylinders. Brake rods, exhausts, piled like snakes, grease, gasoline.

40 Lookin' for a car? What did you have in mind? See anything attracts you? Come on, while your wife's lookin' at that La Salle. You don't want no La Salle. Bearings shot. Uses too much oil. Got a Lincoln '24. There's a car. Run for ever. Make her into a truck.

Hot sun on rusted metal. Oil on the ground.
People are wandering in, bewildered, needing a car.

45 Wipe your feet. Don't lean on that car, it's dirty. How do you buy a car? What does it cost? Watch the children now. I wonder how much for this one? We'll ask. It don't cost money to ask. We can ask, can't we? Can't pay a nickel over seventy-five, or there won't be enough to get to California.

God, if I could only get a hundred jalopies. I don't care if they run or not.

50 Tires: used, bruised tires stacked in tall cylinders; tubes red, grey hanging like sausages.

Tire patch? Radiator cleaner? Spark intensifier? Drop this little pill in your petrol tank and get ten extra miles to the gallon. Just paint it on – you get a new surface for fifty cents. Wipers, fans, belts, gaskets? Maybe it's the valve. Get a new valve stem. What can you lose for a nickel?

55 All right, Joe. You soften 'em up an' shoot 'em in here. I'll close 'em or I'll kill 'em. Don't send in no bums. I want deals.

Yes, sir, step in. You got a buy there. Yes, sir! At eighty bucks you got a buy.

I can't go no higher than fifty. The fella outside says fifty.

60 *Fifty. Fifty*? He's nuts. Paid seventy-eight fifty for that little number, Joe, you crazy fool! Have to can that guy. I might take sixty. Now look here mister, I ain't got all day. I'm a business man. Got anything to trade?

Got a pair of mules I'll trade.

Mules! Hey, Joe, hear this? This guy wants to trade mules. Didn't nobody tell you this is the machine age? They don't use mules for nothing but glue no more.

65 Fine big mules – five and seven years old. Maybe we better look around.

Look around! You come in when we're busy, an' take up our time an' then walk out! Joe, did you know you was talking to pikers?

I ain't a piker. I got to get a car. We're goin' to California. I got to get a car.

70 Well I'm a sucker. Tell you what I'll do. I can get five bucks a piece for them mules for dog feed.

I wouldn't want them to go for dog feed.

Well maybe I can get ten or seven maybe. Tell you what we'll do. We'll take your mules for twenty. Wagon goes with 'em don't it? An' you put up fifty and you can sign a contract to send the rest at ten dollars a month.

75 But you said eighty.

Didn't you never hear about carrying charges and insurance? That just boosts her a little. You'll get her all paid up in four-five months. Sign your name right here. We'll take care of everything.

Well, I don't know –

80 Now look here. I'm giving you my shirt. An' you took all this time. I might a made three sales while I been talkin' to you. I'm disgusted. Yeah, sign right there. All right sir. Joe, fill up the tank for this gentleman. We'll give him petrol.

Jesus, Joe that was a hot one! What'd we give for that jalopy? Thirty bucks – thirty-five wasn't it? I got that team an' if I can't get seventy-five for that team, I ain't a business
85 man. An' I got fifty cash an' a contract for forty more. I know they're not all honest but it'll surprise you how many kick through with the rest.

(From *The Grapes of Wrath* by John Steinbeck, 1939)

Exercise 2.1

Read the extract from *The Grapes of Wrath* and answer the following questions:

1. Who is the main speaker? Why does he use two different styles of speech?

2. Write a paragraph summing up the atmosphere at the 'car lot' – a yard for selling second hand lorries.

3. How does the main speaker bully and take advantage of the customers?

4. There's a lot of American slang in this passage. What do you deduce the following words to mean: (a) screw (line 12), (b) baloney (line 15), (c) lemon (line 30), (d) jerks (line 31), (e) bucks (line 57) and (f) pikers (line 67).

5. Why do you think the author hasn't used speech marks (inverted commas or quotation marks) to show who's speaking?

6. How much profit does the seller make on the vehicle he sells at the end of the passage?

Goblin Market

1   Morning and evening
      Maids heard the goblins cry:
      'Come buy our orchard fruits.
      Come buy, come buy:
5   Apples and quinces,
      Lemons and oranges,
      Plump unpecked cherries,
      Melons and raspberries,
      Bloom-down-cheeked peaches,
10   Swart-headed mulberries,
      Wild free-born cranberries,
      Crab-apples, dewberries,
      Pine-apples, blackberries,
      Apricots, strawberries; –
15   All ripe together
      In summer weather, –
      Morns that pass by.
      Fair eves that fly;
      Come buy, come buy:
20   Pure grapes fresh from the vine,
      Pomegranates full and fine,
      Dates and sharp bullaces,
      Rare pears and greengages,
      Damsons and bilberries,
25   Taste them and try:
      Currants and gooseberries,
      Bright-fire-like barberries,
      Figs to fill the mouth,
      Citrons from the south,
30   Sweet to tongue and sound to eye;
      Come buy, come buy.'

(Opening of 'Goblin Market' by Christina Rossetti, 1862)

Exercise 2.2

Read the poem 'Goblin Market' and answer the following questions:

1.   Reliable refrigeration hadn't been invented when this poem was written. So what is remarkable about this market?

2.   Why are the words 'Come buy' repeated so often?

3. Find examples of the descriptions of the fruit appealing to different senses.

4. In what ways is the atmosphere similar to that of the extract from *The Grapes of Wrath*?

5. What is the effect of the short lines and the rhyming?

Oil price back at US$60 per barrel

1 Oil, sometimes called 'black gold', is vital to the modern world. Specialised equipment pumps it from underground fields. Then it is used for heating and generating electricity. Petrol, diesel and airline fuel are also made from oil.

In 1965 the biggest oil producing countries formed OPEC (Organization of Petroleum
5 Exporting Countries), a cartel to control the quantity of oil produced and its price.

Each OPEC member country may produce only an agreed amount of oil. Oil is measured in barrels – one barrel is 159 litres or 35 gallons. If members produce more the price of oil drops. But if they produce less the price rises.

Because OPEC controls most of the world's oil, it is very powerful.

10 In 1973 Egypt and Syria declared war on Israel. OPEC refused to sell oil to countries that supported Israel – mainly the USA and the countries of Western Europe. The price of oil shot up by 75% to US$90 (at today's prices). So the economies of countries with little or no oil of their own went into recession.

After 1973 new oil fields were developed in the Soviet Union (now Russia), USA,
15 Canada, South East Asia, Norway and the North Sea (off the coast of the UK). That reduced OPEC's power.

The price of oil then remained low for many years. In 2003 it was US$25 per barrel. But by August 2005 it had risen to just over US$70.

The price increased because many countries were consuming more oil. Another factor
20 was that China and India were buying in more and more oil for their fast growing economies.

OPEC still has an important role in fixing oil prices but today the problems are different. In Iraq, Nigeria and Iran – all OPEC member countries – war, civil unrest and worries about United Nations sanctions have reduced the amount of oil they produce. So
25 other OPEC countries are pumping as much oil as they can to meet the demand. The price today is around US$60 per barrel.

If demand continues to rise – but no extra oil is available – the price will rise again to, or above, US$70. Such oil prices could cause problems, as they did in 1973, for the economies of the world's developed countries.

OPEC member countries

Algeria
Indonesia
Iran
Iraq
Kuwait
Libya
Nigeria
Qatar
Saudi Arabia
United Arab Emirates
Venezuela

Over 65% of the world's accessible oil fields are in OPEC countries.

(Slightly adapted from *www.newsademic.com* **an international digital newspaper for 9-16 years olds, 17 March 2006)**

Exercise 2.3

Read the extract from *www.newsademic.com* and answer the following questions:

1. Explain in your own words the meaning of the word 'cartel' (line 5).

2. Why is OPEC so powerful?

3. What reduced OPEC's power after 1973?

4. Why have oil production levels dropped in Iraq, Iran and Nigeria?

5. Which two countries are buying increasing quantities of oil and why?

6. Summarise in your own words why oil prices are rising rapidly now and what effect this is likely to have.

Your turn to write

1. Write a story in which someone is tricked, cheated or conned by someone selling something.

2. Write a colourful description, using as many senses (sight, hearing, touch, taste, smell) as you can to describe any market or shop known to you. You can make your description into a poem if you wish.

3. Imagine you are the customer who buys the lorry at the end of *The Grapes of Wrath* passage. You've got home and had time to think about it. Write your version of what happened.

4.   Today, much selling and marketing takes place, not in shops and markets but over the internet. What do you think about this? What experience of internet shopping do you, and perhaps your family, have? Is it a good development or not? Why? How do you think it will change in the future? Turn your views into an essay about the changing face of shopping.

5.   Write a short essay about the extract from 'Goblin Market'. Comment on the poet's style and use of words. The work you did in Exercise 2.2 will help you.

6.   Write about buying and selling in any way you wish.

Grammar and punctuation

Adverbs

Adverbs are words which modify (qualify) or tell you more about verbs or sometimes about adjectives or participles:

> I read John Steinbeck's novel **quickly**. (adverb 'quickly' modifying verb 'read')
>
> 'Goblin Market' is **colourfully** written. (adverb 'colourfully' qualifying participle 'written')
>
> Oil prices are becoming **alarmingly** high in 2005. (adverb 'alarmingly' telling you more about the adjective 'high')

You will have learned in the past that most adverbs are formed from adjectives and end in '-ly' (e.g. quick/quickly, colourful/colourfully, worrying/worryingly).

Learn now that there are also many adverbs which do NOT end in '-y' and they tend to be those words which can also be adjectives, nouns and verbs in other contexts.

Consider these sentences:

> He sat down on the bank. (Here 'down' is an adverb telling you more about 'sat' but it can also be an adjective in 'down side' or a noun in 'goose down'.)
>
> I ran fast. (Here 'fast' is an adverb modifying 'ran' but it's an adjective in 'fast train' and a noun in 'the fast of Ramadan'. And in 'I fast for Lent' it becomes a verb.)

Exercise 2.4

Use each of the following words as adverbs in sentences of your own:

up   over   well   hard   later

Exercise 2.5

Now use each of the words in Exercise 2.4 in sentences to turn them into as many different parts of speech as you can.

Adverbial clauses of time

Groups of words containing verbs, known as clauses, can do the job of adverbs. Sometimes they answer the question 'when'? These are called **adverbial clauses of time**. Look at these examples:

> Mr Jones read *The Grapes of Wrath* **while he was travelling.** (Qualifies 'read.' Tells us when he read.)

> **Before she died in 1894** Christina Rossetti wrote many poems. (Modifies 'wrote.' Tells us when she wrote.)

> **Once the 1973 war had ended,** oil price sales began to decline. (Tells us more about 'had ended'. Tells us when it had ended.)

Exercise 2.6

Add adverbial clauses of time to these sentences. Such clauses usually begin with 'time' words such as: since, while, during, before, after, as, once. Remember that each clause needs a verb of its own. Think about commas within your sentences too. You may need one to separate the clause from the main sentence.

1.   . . . . John Steinbeck wrote *The Red Pony*.

2.   We read 'Goblin Market' in class . . . .

3.   My mother finished the week's shopping . . . .

4.   . . . . I shall have a rest.

5.   . . . . Sam and Lucy will need their PE kit.

6.   . . . . the oil industry is worried.

Spelling and vocabulary

The signs outside the Oklahoma car sale yard in *The Grapes of Wrath* were 'blazoned'. It means they proclaimed their message very loudly and clearly like a symbol on a coat of arms or family badge. It comes from an old 13th century French word *blason*, a 'coat of arms'.

'Bewildered', which is how the overwhelmed customers felt, comes from a 17th century word meaning 'lost'. The be- prefix means 'caused to be'. The prefix occurs in words like 'betroth', 'betake', 'behove' and 'bedevil' – all words which are no longer used as often as they once were.

Exercise 2.7

Write sentences of your own to show that you understand the meaning of the following verbs:

emblazon   beset   bemuse   belittle   behead   begrudge

Words in gua-

The cars in the John Steinbeck extract are 'guaranteed'. Look carefully at the g-u-a spelling of the word. Other words which have the same construction include:

guacamole
Guadeloupe
guan
guano
guarantor
guard
guardian
Guatemala
guava

(Notice that several of these words come from Spanish in which g-u-a is commoner than in English.)

Exercise 2.8

Match the words above to these definitions. Take great care to spell them correctly:

1.   A tropical fruit.

2.   A person who is bound by a guarantee.

3.   French territory in the Leeward Islands, East Caribbean.

4.   To watch over or shield someone or something from danger.

5.   Droppings of sea birds.

6.   Dip made from avocado, tomato and mayonnaise.

7.   South American bird.

8.   One who looks after or defends.

9.   Country in Central America.

Functions of language

The language of selling

The sellers in *The Grapes of Wrath* and 'Goblin Market' use similar language techniques. They:

- use a lot of imperative verb forms as if they were giving orders ('Come buy', 'Step in', 'Sign your name')
- make the product sound more attractive than it actually is ('There's a car. Run for ever', 'Bloom-down-cheeked peaches')
- sound sincere and passionate
- use language so fast and fluently that it confuses the customer

In addition the main speaker in *The Grapes of Wrath* passage:

- tricks customers into buying something more expensive than they intended to
- lies to the customers, for example about the price he had paid for the vehicles he's selling
- is abusive to his customers when they hesitate
- speaks the truth to his staff so that the reader can see what the dealer is doing

Advertisers today still use many of these techniques although there are laws which prevent them deliberately misleading customers about a product. Sellers are not allowed to browbeat people into buying things, or sign agreements, without allowing them time to think.

Nonetheless many TV advertisements, roadside hoardings, notices in newspapers and magazines and all other forms of advertising use imperative verb forms. And they twist language to make the product sound better than those of its rivals.

Advertising slogans such as 'Beanz Meanz Heinz', 'Let your fingers do the walking' and 'Finger-lickin' good' are interesting too. They use as few words as possible to say something catchy about the product which everyone will remember. People in the advertising industry are paid large sums to think up these slogans.

Exercise 2.9

Write an advertisement for one or more of the following new products. Use the language of selling to make it as persuasive as you can and try to think of a good slogan to go with it:

luminous shoelaces
cake which makes you slim
electric toenail clippers
pig's milk yoghurt

Speaking and listening

1. Working in a group, turn the extract from *The Grapes of Wrath* into a play and perform it to the rest of the class or perhaps in an assembly.

2. Learn the extract from 'Goblin Market' by heart. Practise it until you know exactly how you want to say it. Then demonstrate your work to a partner.

3. Work in a pair. Take turns to tell each other about an occasion when you, or someone in your family, bought or were/was sold something which turned out not to be quite as expected.

4. Work in a pair. One of you is a customer in a shop selling perhaps shoes, flowers or jewellery. The customer should be as awkward as possible. The seller tries to deal with him or her.

5. In a group of three or four talk about the 'science' of selling (or 'marketing') – which can now even be studied as a university subject. How moral do you think it is? Should there be more laws to control it?

Have you read?

These books or plays are either by the writers of the extracts at the beginning of this chapter or they have something to do with selling, shops and sales:

A Single Shard by Linda Sue Park (2001) Oxford University Press
A Kid for Two Farthings by Wolf Mankovitz (1958) Heineman New Windmills
Death of a Salesman by Arthur Miller (1949) Heineman Plays
Hobson's Choice by Harold Brighouse (1915) Heineman Plays
The Hidden Persuaders by Vance Packard (1957) Penguin
East of Eden by John Steinbeck (1952) Penguin Classics
The Old Curiosity Shop by Charles Dickens (1841) Penguin Classics *
Poems of Christina Rossetti – various books available *
The Grapes of Wrath by John Steinbeck (1939) Penguin Classics *
History of Mr Polly by H G Wells (1910) Penguin Classics *

* Recommended for very keen readers and for scholars

And if you've done all that

●   The first Trade Descriptions Act was passed in Britain in the 1960s and there have been many laws to protect consumers since. Find out about these laws, using books and the internet and think about how easy it used to be for buyers to be tricked. What does *caveat emptor* mean?

In this chapter we learned about adverbial clauses of time. Adverbial clauses of place and manner work in a very similar way. Work out what they are and write some sentences using them.

This poem is a song about selling:

I'm called little Buttercup

1   I'm called little Buttercup – dear little Buttercup,
        Though I could never tell why,
     But still I'm called Buttercup – poor little Buttercup
        Sweet little Buttercup I!

5   I've snuff and tobaccy, and excellent jacky[1]
        I've scissors and watches and knives;
     I've ribbons and laces to set off the faces
        Of pretty young sweethearts and wives.

     I've treacle and toffee, I've tea and I've coffee
10   Soft tommy[2] and excellent chops;
     I've chickens and conies and pretty polonies,[3]
        And excellent peppermint drops.

     Then buy of your Buttercup – dear little Buttercup,
        Sailors should never be shy;
15   So buy of your Buttercup – poor little Buttercup;
        Come of your Buttercup buy.

(W S Gilbert, from *HMS Pinafore*, the 1878 operetta he wrote with Sir Arthur Sullivan)

Notes

[1] jacky – twists of tobacco soaked in rum and sold to sailors for chewing
[2] tommy – soft bread usually in the form of fresh rolls
[3] polonies – cold smoked pork sausages. (The word is a corruption of Bologna, the city in Italy where they were first made.)

Look at the rhythm of the song. Say it aloud. It's based on a metric pattern using what are known as anapests: long short short/long short short. What time signature would this be in music? If you don't already know the original song, can you make up, or find, a tune which fits this rhythm?

Chapter 3

Dark days

Charles Dickens (1812-1870) opens one of his most famous novels with a description of a November day in Victorian London.

1   Implacable November weather. As much mud in the streets, as if the waters had but newly retired from the face of the earth, and it would not be wonderful to meet a

5   Megalosaurus, forty feet long or so, waddling like an elephantine lizard up Holborn Hill. Smoke lowering down from chimney-pots, making a soft black drizzle with flakes of soot in it as big as full-grown snowflakes – gone into mourning, one might imagine, for the death of the sun. Dogs, indistinguishable in mire. Horses, scarcely better; splashed to their

10   very blinkers. Foot passengers, jostling one another's umbrellas, in general infection of ill temper, and losing their foot-hold at street-corners, where tens of thousands of other foot passengers have been slipping and sliding since the day broke (if ever this day broke), adding new deposits to the crust of mud, sticking at those points tenaciously to the pavement, and accumulating compound interest.

15   Fog everywhere. Fog up the river, where it flows among green aits[1] and meadows; fog down the river, where it rolls defiled among the tiers of shipping, and the waterside pollutions of a great (and dirty) city. Fog on the Essex marshes, fog on the Kentish heights. Chance people on the bridges peeping over the parapets into a nether sky of fog, with fog all around them, as if they were up in a balloon, and hanging in the misty

20   clouds. Fog creeping into the cabooses of collier-brigs; fog lying out on the yards, and hovering in the rigging of great ships; fog drooping on the gunwales of barges and small boats. Fog in the eyes and throats of ancient Greenwich pensioners, wheezing by the firesides in their wards; fog in the stem and bowl of the afternoon pipe of the wrathful skipper, down in his close cabin; fog cruelly pinching the toes and fingers of his

25   shivering little 'prentice boy on deck.

Gas looming through the fog in divers places in the streets, much as the sun may, from the spongey fields, be seen to loom by husbandman and ploughboy. Most of the shops lighted two hours before their time – as the gas seems to know, for it has a haggard and unwilling look.

(From *Bleak House* by Charles Dickens, 1852)

[1] small islands

Exercise 3.1

Read the extract from *Bleak House* and answer the following questions:

1. What sort of weather is London experiencing? Use your own words to describe it.

2. What do the following words mean (a) tenaciously (line 13), (b) wards (as Dickens uses it here) (line 23) and (c) husbandman (line 27)?

3. Why does Dickens mention a prehistoric animal?

4. What details show that this passage is set in the nineteenth century and not more recently?

5. Explain why the phrase (a metaphor) 'compound interest' (line 14) is appropriate at the beginning of a novel which is going to be mostly about money.

6. How many times does Dickens use the word 'fog' in the second paragraph? Why do you think he repeats it so often?

November

1   The month of the drowned dog. After long rain the land
     Was sodden as the bed of an ancient lake,
     Treed with iron and birdless. In the sunk lane
     The ditch – a seep silent all summer –

5   Made brown foam with a big voice: that, and my boots
     On the lane's scrubbed stones, in the gulleyed leaves,
     Against the hill's hanging silence;
     Mist silvering the droplets on bare thorns

     Slower than the change of daylight.
10   In a let of the ditch a tramp bundled asleep:
     Face tucked down into a beard, drawn in
     Under his hair like a hedgehog's. I took him for dead,

     But his stillness separated him from the death
     Of the rotting grass and the ground. A wind chilled,
15   And a fresh comfort tightened through him,
     Each hand stuffed deeper into the other sleeve.

     His ankles, bound with sacking and hairy band,
     Rubbed each other, resettling. The wind hardened;
     A puff shook a glittering from the thorns,
20   And again the rain's dragging grey columns

Smudged the farms. In a moment
The fields were jumping and smoking; the thorns
Quivered, riddled with the glassy verticals.
I stayed on under the welding cold

25   Watching the tramp's face glisten and the drops on his coat
Flash and darken. I thought what strong trust
Slept in him – as the trickling furrows slept,
And the thorn-roots in their grip on darkness;

And the buried stones, taking the weight of winter;
30   The hill where the hare crouched with clenched teeth.
Rain plastered the land till it was shining
Like hammered lead, and I ran, and in the rushing wood

Shuttered by a black oak leaned.
The keeper's gibbet had owls and hawks
35   By the neck, weasels, a gang of cats, crows:
Some, stiff, weightless, twirled like dry bark bits

In the drilling rain. Some still had their shape,
Had their pride with it; hung, chins on chests,
Patient to outwait these worst days that beat
40   Their crowns bare and dripped from their feet.

(Ted Hughes, 1930-1998)

November

1   No sun – no moon!
No morn – no noon –
No dawn – no dusk – no proper time of day.
No warmth, no cheerfulness, no healthful ease,
5   No comfortable feel in any member –
No shade, no shine, no butterflies, no bees,
No fruits, no flowers, no leaves, no birds! –
November!

(Thomas Hood, 1799-1845)

Exercise 3.2

Read the two poems called 'November' and answer the following questions:

1.   What does Ted Hughes mean by (a) dragging grey columns (line 20) and (b) glassy verticals (line 23)? What do these words tell you about the weather?

2. Describe what the narrator of Ted Hughes's poem sees in a ditch.

3. Choose and comment on three words or phrases which you find interesting in the Ted Hughes poem.

4. What does Ted Hughes's narrator see in the wood?

5. 'Treed' and 'gulleyed' are words which Ted Hughes has invented (or 'coined'). What do they mean and how effective do you think they are?

6. What does Thomas Hood's poem have in common with Ted Hughes's?

7. How do the two poems differ?

8. What does Thomas Hood's poem have in common with the extract from *Bleak House* at the beginning of this chapter?

The following passage is practical advice for British gardeners about November weather:

November's weather: Winter is on its way

1   Leaves are falling rapidly now, and wind and rain are on the increase. Mild spells are possible and the grass may still grow a little in southern England and the Midlands.

Cold snaps are likely, particularly in the second half of the month. Frost, gales, freezing rain and snow are all possible, depending on where you are in the UK. Local
5   topography can make a big difference to weather conditions within a small area. It is worth getting to know your local weather patterns, and gardening accordingly.

Temperature

Although temperatures can be fairly mild this month, it may feel colder than the temperatures suggest. Wind and rain add a chill to the air. In the last three years,
10   temperatures have varied from around 3-5°C (37-41°F) minimum to 8-11.5°C (46-53°F) maximum. But these have been above-average years in terms of warmth. There is always the possibility of a colder year, more in line with past averages.

Night temperatures can occasionally drop to around or below zero, with sudden frosts catching the gardener unaware.

15   The south west of England is often the mildest area at this time of year, and the northern and eastern parts of Scotland can be the coldest. Coastal regions, inland flats and cities are likely to be warmer than hilltops and valleys. The western half of the UK may well be milder than the east.

Rain

20   Rainfall can be very variable at this time of year. November 2004 rainfall was well

below average, 2003 was close to average, and 2002 was generally above average, with major flooding in some areas.

Generally, averages of about 160mm in Scotland, 150mm in Wales, 110mm in Northern Ireland and 80-90mm in England are typical.

25 But regional variations can be marked, and local topography will also create significant differences. The west of Scotland, the coastal parts of Wales and the Lake District of England are some of the wettest regions of the UK, with around 180mm of rain over the month. Parts of south-western England can expect 120-130mm. Eastern Scotland, Northern Ireland and northern England are roughly comparable in rainfall, with around 30 110mm typically in November. The Midlands might expect about 80mm. East Anglia and eastern and central parts of southern England generally have the lowest rainfall, which means 60-70mm being typical for November. However, in a dry November, 45mm might be possible in the South East.

Snow is rare in November, but is much more likely in parts of Scotland, particularly on 35 higher ground.

Wind

Gales are more frequent this month, especially in the Highlands of Scotland, on the Welsh hills, and along the western coasts of England, Wales and Scotland. Northern Ireland is more sheltered, being protected by the westerly parts of the Irish and Scottish land mass.

40 Short gusts up to gale speed can occur anywhere, however, and funnelling effects may worsen conditions even in usually sheltered cities.

Take care when using ladders, when doing any kind of spraying, or when using overhead irrigation systems (in the unlikely event of their being needed).

Sunshine

45 Day length is now short, especially so towards the north of the UK.

The south coast of England has the most sunshine at this time of year, with 65-70 hours being typical for November, but 107 hours being unexceptional in the South West; 59 hours would be more typical for Wales, 45 hours for Scotland and 50 hours for Northern Ireland. Local variations do occur, with some areas being more favoured than others.

50 Hill fogs may reduce visibility in higher areas, and coastal fogs may occasionally be troublesome.

The number of working hours that can be productively spent in the garden is now much reduced. You may wish to think about installing lighting in the garden, shed or greenhouse, to increase productivity or simply to enjoy the view out from cosy windows.

(Advice on website of The Royal Horticultural Society *www.rhs.org.uk*)

Exercise 3.3

Read the extract from The Royal Horticultural Society website and answer the following questions:

1. Which parts of Britain are usually the driest in November?

2. Why are gardeners advised to take extra care when working above ground level in November?

3. Why do you think it is difficult for gardeners if they are caught unaware by sudden frost?

4. Whereabouts in Britain is the coldest November weather likely?

5. What happened in November 2002 which was unusual?

6. What are (a) topography (line 5), (b) irrigation (line 43) and (c) productivity (line 54)?

Your turn to write

1. Write a story or poem entitled 'November'.

2. Imagine you are the sleeping tramp in Ted Hughes's poem. Tell your story.

3. You are an advice columnist in a magazine or newspaper. A reader writes saying that he or she finds November a very dull month and can think of nothing to do. Write your answer.

4. Write the next three or four paragraphs to follow Dickens's description in the extract from *Bleak House* given above. Remember he is about to introduce some characters and/or action. Try to use his style if you can.

5. Write about November or Dark Days in any way you wish.

6. 'How does Dickens make the opening of *Bleak House* interesting?' Answer this question as an English literature essay. Comment on Dickens's use of language and pick out phrases and words which you find particularly interesting. Your answers to Exercise 3.1 will help you.

Grammar and punctuation

Modifiers

A **modifier** is a word or phrase which modifies, transforms, changes, alters, qualifies, determines or affects the meaning of another word or phrase.

Modifiers, which are sometimes called determiners, include various sorts of adjective and adjectival phrases, adverbs and adverbial phrases, articles and possessive pronouns.

Consider these examples. The modifier is in bold.

She wore a hat

She wore **your** hat (possessive pronoun modifies 'hat')

She wore a hat, **inherited from her grandmother** (adjectival phrase modifies 'hat')

We waited

We waited **quietly** (adverb modifies 'waited')

We waited **in quiet respect** (adverbial phrase modifies 'waited')

Children laugh

Some children laugh (adjective modifies 'children')

Books are entertaining

These books are entertaining (adjective modifies 'books' but note that if we simply said 'these' and dropped 'books' it would become a pronoun)

Teachers were in the staff room

The teachers were in the staff room (definite article modifies 'teachers')

In each case the modifier changes the meaning of the sentence.

Modifiers are a large group. Think of them as a big grammatical 'file' into which many smaller files fit.

Exercise 3.4

Put modifiers, which can be single words or phrases, into the gaps in these sentences. (Note each sentence already makes sense but you are changing the meaning.)

1. Charles Dickens wrote _____ books.

2. November, December, January and February are _____ months.

3. Richard ate _____ .

4. _____ , Thomas Hood was a _____ poet.

5. I like _____ poems _____ plays and _____ fiction.

6. _____ modifiers are adjectives and adverbs.

7. Would you like to have _____ supper with us _____ ?

8. There is _____ difficulty here.

9. I like _____ cooking.

10. _____ music is _____ too loud.

Revision of apostrophes

Remember that apostrophes have two functions:

> They stand in place of omitted letters

> They indicate possession

Look at these examples from the passages at the beginning of this chapter:

omission

> 'prentice boy (for **ap**prentice boy)

possession

> one another's umbrellas

> the tramp's face

> the hill's hanging silence

> the keeper's gibbet

> like a hedghog's (hair)

But notice there are many words used in the passages which do not, of course, need an apostrophe because there is no omission or possession: 'snowflakes', 'marshes', 'leaves', 'butterflies'.

One of the worst mistakes you can make is to put an apostrophe simply because the word is plural.

Exercise 3.5

Put apostrophes in these examples where they are needed. In brackets after each put (p) for possession, (o) for omission or (n) for no apostrophe needed:

1. Thomas Hoods poems

2. dos and donts

3. novels written by Victorians

4. St Marys Church

5. the reigns of Stuart Kings and Queens

6.   Queen Annes reign

7.   six oclock

8.   the witnesss statement

9.   we shouldnt

10.   the foxs habitat

11.   Guys and Dolls

12.   Aunt Glyniss house

Semi-colons for lists

Look carefully at the punctuation in these sentences from *Bleak House*:

> Fog creeping into the cabooses of collier-brigs; fog lying out on the yards, and hovering in the rigging of great ships; fog drooping on the gunwales of barges and small boats.

> Fog in the eyes and throats of ancient Greenwich pensioners, wheezing by the firesides in their wards; fog in the stem and bowl of the afternoon pipe of the wrathful skipper, down in his close cabin; fog cruelly pinching the toes and fingers of his shivering little 'prentice boy on deck.

Dickens is using semicolons to divide items in lists in long sentences. A semicolon is stronger than a comma, so if complex items are being listed the writer can use commas as subdividers inside the items in the list – although not always. And it is all, of course, inside the usual sentence 'box' with a capital letter at the beginning and a full stop at the end. As with commas for lists you don't need a semicolon if you use 'and', 'but' or 'or' before the final listed item. There is no capital letter after a semicolon unless the word is a proper noun or other word which needs a capital letter in its own right.

For example:

The mouse found nuts, berries and seeds; it buried them in cavities in bark, inside the debris of the greenhouse and under rocks; revisited its stashes, ensured the security of the hoards and made final coverings and, during winter dearths, searched them out again.

Exercise 3.6

Use semicolons to divide the items listed in these sentences:

1.   I bought oranges, because they are my mother's favourite and she has a bad cold bananas for Peter some fresh dates, which we all like unripe peaches, which will be ready in a few days and a big bag of overripe apples for my horse, who loves them for treats.

2.   Our tour of America took us to New England where Dad was fascinated by Boston and

its history into California where we didn't like Los Angeles but loved the countryside eastward along the Mexican border eventually to Louisiana and Alabama and included highlights like Charleston in South Carolina.

3.   This year Yasmin has already read three books by Charles Dickens, which she says she enjoyed very much most of Daphne du Maurier, including *The Glass Blowers* four modern crime novels biographies of William Pitt and Charles Darwin and quite a lot of poetry.

Spelling and vocabulary

'Horticulture' comes from the Latin words *hortus* a 'garden' and *cultura* 'growing'. Horticulture is therefore the art of cultivating gardens. 'Horticultural' is the adjective which stems from it and a 'horticulturalist' is another word for a gardener.

Exercise 3.7

Give definitions for the following words ending in '-culture':

agriculture   viticulture   silviculture   apiculture   monoculture   aquaculture

'Topography' comes from the Ancient Greek word *topos*, 'a place'. Other English words from the same root are:

topology: the study of geometrical properties

toponym: a place name such as Hampstead or Weston-on-the-Green

toponymy: the study of place names

A number of words in English end in '-onym' meaning 'name' (see below).

Exercise 3.8

Find the meanings (if you don't already know them) of the following '-onym' words and use them in sentences of your own:

pseudonym   acronym   cryptonym   eponym   synonym   metonym

Look carefully at the spelling of 'irrigation' with its double 'r'.

The following words also have a double 'r':

irritation, barrister, correspond, embarrass, quarrelsome, Mediterranean, occurring, overripe.

Exercise 3.9

Make a list of as many other words as you can which have a double 'r'.

Functions of language

Breaking the rules

In the extract Dickens has written entirely in sentence fragments – part sentences which don't have a formal subject and verb. They are not therefore grammatically 'correct'.
We saw Daphne du Maurier using this technique in Chapter 1, but Dickens has taken it further.

Examples:

- Implacable November weather.
- Dogs, indistinguishable in mire.
- Fog everywhere.

This is quite easy to spot in very short sentences, but if you look carefully at the passage you will see that the longer sentences are fragments too:

- Gas looming through the fog in divers places in the streets, much as the sun may, from the spongey fields, be seen to loom by husbandman and ploughboy.
- As much mud in the streets, as if the waters had but newly retired from the face of the earth, and it would not be wonderful to meet a Megalosaurus, forty feet long or so, waddling like an elephantine lizard up Holborn Hill.

The effect of this is to make Dickens's observations read like notes. (Don't forget he was a journalist as well as a novelist.) It's a style associated with very personal, impressionistic writing – in diaries for example. And it allows Dickens to start as many sentences as he likes with that plodding, heavy-sounding word 'fog'. If he'd carefully observed the rules of grammar and written 'There was fog everywhere', or 'Fog was everywhere', the impact would have been slower, duller and much less immediate.

One of the differences between poetry and prose is that poems tend to use sentence fragments rather than grammatical sentences. For example:

> Face tucked down into a beard, drawn in
> Under his hair like a hedgehog's.

> No sun – no moon!

This is why Dickens's description of London feels quite poetic as well as vivid.

Exercise 3.10

Write out a section of the *Bleak House* extract, setting it out on the page as if it were a poem. Remember that poems usually begin each new line with a capital letter so you may need to adjust Dickens's punctuation. Would you have known, if you'd seen your version in a poetry book, that it wasn't written as a poem? Explain your answer.

Exercise 3.11

Write a paragraph describing a scene you know well using only sentence fragments. (If you are using a computer, the grammar check will not approve of this exercise – ignore it on this occasion.)

There is nothing wrong with breaking grammatical rules when you're writing creatively provided that you understand exactly what you're doing, know why you're doing it and do it with flair – Dickens knew the rules of grammar as well as anyone!

Speaking and listening

1. Learn the Thomas Hood poem by heart and practise saying it.

2. In groups of about four discuss your experience of, and feelings about, November. All the extracts in this chapter regard it rather negatively. Is there anything that you *like* about November?

3. Imagine you are a television newsreader. Report on the weather in London in an appropriate style for the November day that Dickens describes at the beginning of *Bleak House*. (Imagination is needed here. Of course there was no TV in 1852. Use a modern TV style but take your weather information from the passage.)

4. Organise a class debate on the proposition 'This house thinks that winter is more enjoyable than summer'.

5. Work in a pair. Take it in turns to tell each other about the best book you have read in the last three months.

Have you read?

These books are either connected with the extracts at the beginning of this chapter or they relate in some ways to the theme of dark days:

The Hobbit by J R R Tolkien (1937) HarperCollins
Darker plays by Shakespeare such as *King Lear*, *Othello* and *Hamlet*. *Shakespeare Stories* (1985) *and Shakespeare Stories II* (1994) by Leon Garfield are a good starting point.
The Fire-eaters by David Almond (2003) Hodder
The Foreshadowing by Marcus Sedgewick (2005) Orion
Collected Poems of Ted Hughes Faber and Faber
Selected Poems of Thomas Hood Fyfield Books
A Town like Alice by Nevil Shute (1950) House of Stratus
Plant by David Burnie (2003) Dorling Kindersley Eye Witness Guides
Bleak House by Charles Dickens (1852) Penguin *
Little Dorrit by Charles Dickens (1857) Wordsworth Classics *
Jude the Obscure by Thomas Hardy (1895) Oxford World's Classics *
Heart of Darkness by Joseph Conrad (1902) Penguin Popular Classics *

* Recommended for very keen readers and for scholars

And if you've done all that

- Find out why fogs – which used to be nicknamed 'pea-soupers' because they were a thick greyish green and you couldn't see through them – were so much worse in 1852 than they are today. Write a paragraph about this and keep it to refer to.

- Look at the Royal Horticultural Society's website. You will see that the Society does a lot of work with schools and for education. Is there anything which your school could – if your teachers agreed – get involved in? Could your class, for example, visit the Society's headquarters at Wisley in Surrey or one of its gardens in other parts of the country?

- Seasonal Affective Disorder (SAD) is a recognised mental health problem and it is probably commonest in November. Find out what you can about it. Do you know anyone who suffers from it? What could you – or anyone else – do to help?

- During autumn 2005 the BBC ran a new serialisation of *Bleak House* which many people liked very much. It was issued on DVD (3 discs) in February 2006. Watch this (again, if you've seen it before) so that you know the outline story. Then try reading the book.

Chapter 4

People who aren't what they seem

Mr Slope is chaplain, a personal assistant, to the newly appointed Bishop Proudie in nineteenth century Barchester, an imaginary city in the west of England. He is not exactly a hero.

1   Mr Slope is tall, and not ill made. His feet and hands are large, as has ever been the case with all his family, but he has a broad chest and wide shoulders to carry off these excrescences, and on the whole his figure is good. His countenance, however, is not specially prepossessing. His hair is lank, and of a dull pale reddish hue. It is always

5   formed into three straight lumpy masses, each brushed with admirable precision, and cemented with much grease; two of them adhere closely to the sides of his face, and the other lies at right angles above them. He wears no whiskers, and is always punctiliously shaven. His face is nearly the same colour as his hair, though perhaps a little redder: it is not unlike beef – beef, however, one would say of bad quality. His forehead is capacious

10   and high, but square and heavy, and unpleasantly shining. His mouth is large, though his lips are thin and bloodless; and his big, prominent, pale brown eyes inspire everything except confidence. His nose, however, is his redeeming feature: it is pronounced, straight, and well-formed; though I myself should have liked it better did it not possess a somewhat spongy, porous appearance, as though it had been cleverly formed out of a

15   red coloured cork.

I never could endure to shake hands with Mr Slope. A cold, clammy perspiration always exudes from him, the small drops are even seen standing on his brow, and his friendly grasp is unpleasant.

20 Such is Mr Slope – such is the man who has suddenly fallen into the midst of Barchester Close, and is destined there to assume the station which had hitherto been filled by the son of the late bishop. Think, oh, my meditative reader, what an associate we have here for those comfortable prebendaries, those gentlemanlike clerical doctors, those happy, well-used, well-fed minor canons, who have grown into existence at Barchester under the kindly wings of Bishop Grantly!

25 But not as mere associate for these does Mr Slope travel down to Barchester with the bishop and his wife. He intends to be, if not their master, at least the chief among them. He intends to lead, and to have followers; he intends to hold the purse strings of the diocese, and draw around him an obedient herd of his poor and hungry brethren.

(From *Barchester Towers* by Anthony Trollope, 1857)

Exercise 4.1

Read the extract from *Barchester Towers* and answer the following questions:

1. Summarise Mr Slope's appearance in your own words.

2. What is the name of the previous bishop and what can you deduce about the attitude of Barchester clergy to him?

3. Who had been chaplain to the previous bishop?

4. What do you learn about Mr Slope's attitude to his new job from this passage?

5. Give other words or phrases for (a) excrescences (line 3), (b) punctiliously (line 7), (c) capacious (line 9) and (d) prebendaries (line 22).

6. What impression does the author want the reader to have of Mr Slope?

This poem, set in 16th century Italy, was written in 1842:

My Last Duchess

1 That's my last duchess painted on the wall,
   Looking as if she were alive. I call
   That piece a wonder, now: Frà Pandolf's hands
   Worked busily a day, and there she stands.
5 Will't please you sit and look at her? I said
   'Frà Pandolf' by design, for never read
   Strangers like you that pictured countenance,
   The depth and passion of its earnest glance,
   But to myself they turned (since none puts by
10 The curtain I have drawn for you, but I)
   And seemed as they would ask me, if they durst,

How such a glance came there; so, not the first
Are you to turn and ask thus. Sir, 'twas not
Her husband's presence only, called that spot
15 Of joy into the Duchess' cheek: perhaps
Frà Pandolf chanced to say, 'Her mantle laps
Over my lady's wrist too much,' or 'Paint
Must never hope to reproduce the faint
Half-flush that dies along her throat': such stuff
20 Was courtesy, she thought, and cause enough
For calling up that spot of joy. She had
A heart – how shall I say? – too soon made glad,
Too easily impressed; she liked whate'er
She looked on, and her looks went everywhere.
25 Sir, 'twas all one! My favour at her breast,
The dropping of the daylight in the West,
The bough of cherries some officious fool
Broke in the orchard for her, the white mule
She rode with round the terrace – all and each
30 Would draw from her alike the approving speech,
Or blush, at least. She thanked men – good! but thanked
Somehow – I know not how – as she ranked
My gift of a nine-hundred-years-old name
With anybody's gift. Who'd stoop to blame
35 This sort of trifling? Even had you skill
In speech – (which I have not) – to make your will
Quite clear to such an one, and say, 'Just this
Or that in you disgusts me; here you miss,
Or there exceed the mark' – and if she let
40 Herself be lessoned so, nor plainly set
Her wits to yours, forsooth, and made excuse,
Never to stoop. Oh sir, she smiled, no doubt,
Whene'er I passed her; but who passed without
Much the same smile? This grew; I gave commands;
45 Then all smiles stopped together. There she stands
As if alive. Will't please you rise? We'll meet
The company below, then. I repeat
The Count your master's known munificence
Is ample warrant that no just pretence
50 Of mine for dowry will be disallowed;
Though his fair daughter's self, as I avowed
At starting, is my object. Nay, we'll go
Together down sir. Notice Neptune, though,
Taming a sea-horse, thought a rarity,
55 Which Claus of Innsbruck cast in bronze for me!

(Robert Browning, 1842)

Exercise 4.2

Read the poem 'My Last Duchess' and answer the following questions:

1. Who is the narrator of the poem?

2. Whom is the narrator addressing and what is he negotiating for?

3. What has happened to 'my last duchess'?

4. Chose and list three or four words or phrases which emphasise the sinister power of the narrator.

5. Why does the speaker mention the sculpture of Neptune at the end?

6. What does rhyme contribute to this poem?

Lost portrait of Mozart reveals bloated result of years of drinking and womanising

1   A newly discovered and unflattering portrait of Wolfgang Amadeus Mozart, painted in 1790 just a year before his death at the age of 34, has revealed for the first time the impact on his looks of the composer's louche way of life.

Despite the tendency at the time for artists to enhance their subjects, increasing the
5   chance of collecting their fee, the painting shows a greying and podgy Mozart, with heavy bags under his eyes, who looks much older than 34 – and a far cry from the impish prodigy often featured on Austrian tourist brochures.

His flamboyant living in his home town of Salzburg revolved around rich foods, heavy drinking and womanising, all of which may have contributed to his premature death in
10   Vienna while he was working on a Requiem Mass.

The 32in by 25in oil painting by Johann Georg Edlinger, a German artist, belongs to the Berlin Picture Gallery. It was bought in 1934 for 650 reichsmarks but later forgotten about and lay collecting dust in the museum's storage depot.

One of only ten portraits in existence, it was recently rediscovered and authenticated by
15   Wolfgang Seiller, an authority on Mozart and distant relative of the composer.

He alerted the gallery's chief curator, Dr Rainer Michaelis, who ordered tests which concluded that the painting was of Mozart. Computer comparisons were made between the painting and a previously authenticated portrait, painted 13 years earlier, which hangs in the Museum of Music in Bologna, Italy.

20   'Mr Seiller noticed the strong similarities between the person in the painting and Mozart. It was only then that we decided to do a thorough investigation,' said Dr

Michaelis. 'The computer compared the faces: the eyes, the nose, everything matched up, and confirms this is the last known portrait of Mozart. There is no doubt.'

He said that the puffiness of Mozart's face could have been the result of his being
25   treated with mercury. He is believed to have died of kidney failure or syphilis.

Historians believe that Mozart sat for the portrait during his last visit to Munich, when he stayed at his favourite inn, the *At the Black Eagle*. The owner of the inn was a close friend of both Mozart and the artist, Edlinger, and they are believed to have met there.

The portrait has been fully restored by the museum's chief restorer, Ute Stehr, and will
30   be put on public display on January 27, the 249th anniversary of Mozart's birth.

Walter Hauser, a musician in Salzburg, defended his hero's reputation. 'Mozart had a lot of enemies,' Mr Hauser said. 'I would not be surprised if the artist was asked to paint an unflattering picture for some long-forgotten political motive, probably long after his death. There were many people jealous of Mozart's talent.'

(Bojan Pancevski, *The Daily Telegraph***, 9 January 2006)**

Exercise 4.3

Read the above extract and answer the following questions:

1. Explain the meanings of (a) louche (line 3), (b) prodigy (line 7) and (c) authenticated (line 14).

2. Describe the newly discovered painting in your own words and explain why it has surprised people.

3. Where and how was the newly discovered portrait found?

4 How do the experts know that the painting is genuine?

5. Summarise Walter Hauser's view of the painting. Use your own words.

Your turn to write

1. Imagine you are the Count's daughter who is to be married to the Duke in Browning's poem. Write an entry for your diary describing your first meeting with the man your father has decided you will marry.

2. Write a story entitled 'Not exactly a hero'.

3. You are the daughter or son of a clergyman in Barchester. Mr Slope comes to tea and it's the first time you have met him. Write your impressions; use your imagination to add to the information in the passage.

4. Write a letter to *The Daily Telegraph* commenting on, or stating your views about, the newly discovered Mozart portrait.

5. Write an essay about 'My Last Duchess'. Mention the story that the poem tells, how it is told and the way the poet gets his effects. Make sure you comment in detail on some of Browning's words and phrases. You can use some of your answers to Exercise 4.2 as a starting point. And the notes in the Functions of Language section later in this chapter (page 50) could help you.

6. Write in any way you wish about people who aren't what they seem.

Grammar and punctuation

Anticipatory phrases

Look at the phrases which open these sentences:

> **One of only ten portraits in existence**, it was recently rediscovered and authenticated by Wolfgang Seiller.

> **Written in the mid-nineteenth century**, Robert Browning's poem tells a 16th century story.

Each is an anticipatory phrase. That means that it looks ahead to something, which is yet to come in the sentence. Unless something is added the phrase would be meaningless.

The phrase 'One of only ten portraits in existence' relates to the pronoun 'it' (the portrait of Mozart) which comes next. The phrase 'written in the mid-nineteenth century' relates to 'Robert Browning's poem'. In both cases the opening phrase anticipates the subject of the sentence.

This is a neat, useful and elegant device in writing because it helps to vary sentence shape and means fewer sentences repetitively beginning with the subject. It can enable a point to be well made in fewer words too.

But it's easy to get it wrong. In English, word order (syntax) affects meaning. It is important that the subject, which the phrase is referring to comes immediately after the anticipatory phrase, otherwise the sentence makes no sense or means something other than the writer intends.

For example:

> One of only ten portraits in existence, Mr Seiller found it. (Mr Seiller is not a portrait.)

> Written in the nineteenth century, Robert Browning wrote his poem in Florence. (Robert Browning was not written in the nineteenth century.)

Exercise 4.4

Look carefully at these sentences. Some are correct and some are not. Correct (or alter so that they make sense) the ones which are wrong. You may need to change words as well as word order.

1. Always tasty at Pizza Express, I enjoyed lunch.

2. A part-time novelist, Anthony Trollope also worked for the Post Office.

3. Much admired by generations of concertgoers, Mozart was born in 1756.

4. Her voice very dramatic, the class listened while Fiona read her poem.

5. Falling on 14th February, lovers the world over celebrate St Valentine's Day.

6. Inspired by Robert Browning, a poem a day was Andrew's goal.

Revision of apostrophes for possessive plurals

Remember, in English we use an apostrophe followed by 's' to show possession. The apostrophe and 's' come immediately after the word that is possessing (e.g. 'Paul's friend', 'my sister's dog'). If the possessor is plural, the rule is the same except that we do not add 's' after the apostrophe if the plural possessor already ends in 's' (which of course it normally does).

Thus:

> girls' books (several girls in possession of books)
>
> ladies' shoes (shoes belonging to more than one lady)
>
> actresses' scripts (several actresses in possession of scripts)
>
> foxes' lairs (several foxes in possession of lairs)

Note, however, that if the plural possessor does **not** end in 's', we add apostrophe and 's' as normal. Thus:

> men's shoes (shoes belonging to more than one man)
>
> geese's feathers (feathers belonging to more than one goose)

Exercise 4.5

1. Write these words as plural possessives:

    | baby | princess | ibex | church | fairy | teacher |
    | headmistress | bush | scientist | musician | army | author |
    | country | grandmother | granny | | | |

2. Now put each one of these plural possessives into a sentence of your own.

Spelling and vocabulary

Heteronyms

Look at these sentences:

> Browning makes his Duke refuse to stoop.
>
> It is lucky that the Edlinger's portrait of Mozart was not put out with the refuse.
>
> Mr Slope is keen to present his views to everyone he meets in Barchester.
>
> If Mr Slope visits a lady he usually takes a little present with him.

'Refuse' and 'refuse' look identical when written so we have to deduce what they mean from their context. In speech they sound different because we stress them differently with our voices.

If we mean to refuse to do something we say re**fuse**. If we mean rubbish we say **re**fuse. Pre**sent** and **pre**sent are another example.

These pairs of words are called **heteronyms**.

Exercise 4.6

Write two sentences to illustrate the use of each of the following heteronymns:

invalid	minute	second	collect	contract
digest	viola	console	rejoin	process

Heteronyms are quite common in English because ours is a stressed language. You can change the meaning or function of a word by stressing different parts of it too.

For example pro**duce** and sub**ject** are verbs. **Prod**uce and **subj**ect are nouns.

Exercise 4.7

Write sentences using the following words. The stressed syllable is highlighted to help you:

fre**quent** (verb)   **con**vict (noun)   **reb**el (noun)   con**test** (verb)

ab**sent** (verb)   **con**duct (noun)

Sometimes we move the stress when we add prefixes and suffixes to words too. For example, we say **illu**strate but illu**strat**ion, **strat**egy but stra**teg**ic, **mem**ory but me**mor**ial and ap**pear** but **dis**appear.

This is an aspect of English that many people learning it as an acquired language find very difficult. For those of us who grew up speaking and hearing English it usually comes instinctively, but you need to be aware of the tricks the language is playing.

The silent p

Some words in English begin with a 'p' which is not pronounced. They come from Greek and they just have to be learned. Thus:

Psychiatrist comes from the Greek words *psyche* = mind and *iatros* = doctor.

For the next exercise, the following will be useful:

psōra	an itchy disease
ptōchos	beggarly, poor
pseudēs	false, untrue
psalmos	a song sung to a stringed instrument
pteris	a feathery fern
pneuma	wind, air
pneumōn	lungs
pteron	feather
ptōsis	falling

Exercise 4.8

1. Link these definitions with the right meanings:

air filled (e.g. a tyre)	psoriasis
extinct flying reptile	ptochocracy
poetic prayer, often sung	ptosis
doctor who treats mental illness	pseudo
serious lung infection	psalm
drooping of upper eye lid	pteridology
skin disease	psychiatrist
false	pneumonia
study of ferns	pterodactyl
government by the poor	pneumatic

2. Now learn the spellings and meanings of these ten words if you don't already know them.

And lastly . . . . if you use 'Never Eat Shredded Wheat' to remember the points of the compass or **BIDMAS** (**B**rackets, **I**ndex numbers, **D**ivide, **M**ultiply, **A**dd, **S**ubtract) to help you remember the order in which you should tackle maths calculations, you are using a **mnemonic** or memory aid. The 'm' is silent and mnemonic is a very unusual word. Make sure you can spell it. We get the word from **Mnemosyne** who was the goddess of memory and the mother of Zeus in Ancient Greek mythology.

3. List eight different silent 'p' words by using a dictionary to help you. Then make sure you know the meanings and spellings of all the words on your list.

Functions of language

Spelling out a subtext

Anthony Trollope's Mr Slope is very unappealing to look at and the reader understands that he isn't very nice to know either. But Trollope doesn't tell you any of this directly. He implies it.

In 'My Last Duchess', Browning is presenting a monologue in verse. The speaker is a ruthless murderer. But, like Trollope, Browning makes his meaning very clear by implication rather than by what is actually said.

Conveying ideas by implication rather than by stating them outright is known as **subtext**. Playwrights use it in drama when characters don't say what they actually mean but the audience knows what is going on in their minds because of gesture and tone. Novelists and poets do something similar and the term has been borrowed from drama to describe it.

Trollope:

- praises Mr Slope sparingly to suggest that he's being very fair (his nose and his figure)
- uses a lot of negatives to tone down his comments rather than choosing the vocabulary of obvious dislike ('not ill made', 'no whiskers', 'not especially prepossessing')
- chooses humorous imagery expressed with pretend seriousness (bad beef, red cork)
- repeats for emphasis (intends)
- addresses the reader directly as if we and he are friends sharing a confidential chat ('Oh, my meditative reader', 'I never could')

Browning:

- makes the duke speak very politely ('Will't please you rise?')
- ensures that the duke is very fluent and convincing – obviously in charge
- gives the duke very simple vocabulary so that there can be no misunderstanding ('She had / A heart – how shall I say? – too soon made glad')
- never uses direct words like kill, destroy or murder
- conveys power obliquely ('My gift of a nine-hundred-years-old name')
- has the duke speak chillingly ('There she stands /As if alive')

Exercise 4.9

Re read the extract from *Barchester Towers*. Write a short summary of Trollope's subtext. What, in plain, blunt language, is he trying to tell us about Mr Slope?

Exercise 4.10

Re read 'My Last Duchess'. Summarise in a paragraph exactly what the Duke is telling the visitor. Be as direct as you can.

Speaking and listening

1. Read one of the books listed in the next section. Tell a partner about the book, doing your utmost to persuade him or her to read it too.

2. Prepare a reading of the description of Mr Slope. Make it as lively and interesting as you can, remembering to communicate what you think the author really feels.

3. Work in a small group. Discuss 'My Last Duchess'. Make sure that the points you all make relate to the words of the poem. Decide how much you like the poem as a piece of writing and why.

4. Work in a pair. One of you is Mr Slope. The other is a lady he is visiting in Barchester. It is the first time he has called. Role play the conversation.

5. Prepare a short talk for the class about an interesting character either known to you or from history or from fiction.

Have you read?

These books either relate to the extracts at the beginning of this chapter or they include people or situations which aren't quite what they seem:

Going for Stone by Philip Gross (2002) OUP
The Shell House by Linda Newberry (2002) Red Fox
Scarecrows by Robert Westall (1981) Definitions
Postcards from No-man's Land by Aidan Chambers (1998) Speak
The Poems of Robert Browning, Wordsworth Poetry Library
Hester's Story by Adèle Géras (2004) Orion
Nineteen Eighty Four by George Orwell (1948) Penguin Modern Classics
Never Let Me Go by Kazuo Ishiguro (2005) Faber & Faber *
Barchester Towers by Anthony Trollope (1857) Oxford World Classics *
The Warden by Anthony Trollope (1855) Oxford World Classics *

* Recommended for very keen readers and for scholars

And if you've done all that

●   In the 1980s the BBC serialised *Barchester Towers* and another book in the same series by Anthony Trollope, *The Warden*. Alan Rickman is excellent as Mr Slope. Titled *The Barchester Chronicles* it is available on both video and DVD. Watch it so that you know the outline story. Then try reading the books.

●   Robert Browning (1812-1889) married another poet Elizabeth Barrett (1806-1861), known after their wedding in 1846 as Elizabeth Barrett Browning. The story of their courtship and marriage is pretty remarkable. Find out about their lives and read some (more) of the poetry they each wrote.

●   Listen to some of Mozart's symphonies, concertos and other pieces and find out from books and the internet about his life. Prepare a short presentation about him for the rest of the class using some of the music to illustrate your talk.

Chapter 5

Beauty

This is a 1579 translation by Sir Thomas North of part of Lives *by Plutarch, a Greek biographer who lived between approximately 50 and 120 A.D. It describes Cleopatra setting out to meet Mark Antony.*

1   She disdained to set forward otherwise but to take her barge in the river of Cydnus, the poop whereof was of gold, the sails of purple, and the oars of silver, which kept stroke in rowing after the sound of the music of flutes, howboys, citherns, viols and other such instruments as they played upon the barge. And now for the person herself: she was laid
5   under a pavilion of cloth of gold of tissue, apparelled and attired like the goddess Venus commonly drawn in picture; and hard by her, on either hand of her, pretty fair boys apparelled as painters do set forth god Cupid, with little fans in their hands, with which they fanned wind upon her.

(from *Lives* by Thomas North)

Here is Shakespeare's version as it appears in his 1607 play *Antony and Cleopatra*:

1   The barge she sat in, like a burnished throne
       Burned on the water. The poop was beaten gold;
       Purple were the sails, and so perfumèd that
       The winds were lovesick with them. The oars were silver,
5   Which to the tune of flutes kept stroke, and made
       The water which they beat to follow faster,
       As amorous of their strokes. For her own person,
       It beggared all description: she did lie
       In her pavilion – cloth of gold, of tissue –
10   O'erpicturing that Venus where we see
       The fancy outwork nature. On each side her
       Stood pretty dimpled boys, like smiling Cupids,
       With divers-coloured fans, whose wind did seem
       To glow the delicate cheeks which they did cool,
15   And what they undid did.

(from *Antony and Cleopatra* by William Shakespeare, 1607)

Exercise 5.1

Read the above extracts from the translation by Sir Thomas North and Shakespeare's *Antony and Cleopatra* and answer the following questions:

1. What is the most obvious difference between these two pieces of writing?

2. Which river was Cleopatra's barge sailing on?

3. How was the barge driven?

4. What has Shakespeare taken directly from Plutarch, his source, and what has he added?

5. From Shakespeare's lines explain the meaning of (a) 'It beggared all description' (line 8) and (b) 'And what they undid did' (line 15).

6. Which of these two descriptions do you prefer and why?

The Wild Swans at Coole

<pre>
1   The trees are in their autumn beauty,
       The woodland paths are dry,
       Under the October twilight the water
       Mirrors a still sky;
5   Upon the brimming water among the stones
       Are nine-and-fifty swans.

       The nineteenth autumn has come upon me
       Since I first made my count;
       I saw, before I had well finished,
10   All suddenly mount
       And scatter wheeling in great broken rings
       Upon their clamorous wings.

       I have looked upon these brilliant creatures,
       And now my heart is sore.
15   All's changed since I, hearing at twilight,
       The first time on this shore,
       The bell-beat of their wings above my head,
       Trod with a lighter tread.

       Unwearied still, lover by lover,
20   They paddle in the cold
       Companionable streams or climb the air;
       Their hearts have not grown old;
       Passion or conquest, wander where they will,
       Attend upon them still.
</pre>

25   But now they drift on the still water,
      Mysterious, beautiful;
      Among what rushes will they build,
      By what lake's edge or pool
      Delight men's eyes when I wake some day
30   To find they have flown away?

(W B Yeats, 1917)

Exercise 5.2

Read the poem 'The Wild Swans At Coole' and answer the following questions:

1.   For how long has the narrator been observing the swans?

2.   What time of year and what time of day is it?

3.   How many birds are there?

4.   Which words and phrases describe the sound of the swans?

5.   In what way does he find them beautiful?

6.   What is the mood of the poem?

Hair today and gone tomorrow

1   All cities have lots of them. Like mushrooms they spring up when no one's looking.
      Once they were simply called hairdressers or barbers but today they use pretentious
      vocabulary borrowed from other professions and life styles. 'Treatments' are
      recommended in 'salons' by 'hair consultants', 'designers' or 'stylists'.

5   In their expensively fitted-out shops, punningly named things like 'Prime Cuts', 'Hair
      and Now' or 'Head Line' city hairdressers are getting above themselves in a big way.
      Their premises are deliberately made to look like up-market clinics (without being
      clinical of course) with the staff in white uniforms, faintly reminiscent of nurses.
      Hairdressers, let it not be forgotten, are the descendants of servants – ladies' maids and
10   the like. They are not related to professions like medicine.

      And what happens when you get inside these hairdressers' shops? The client – they have
      yet to call the customers 'patients' but it won't be long – submits, at considerable
      expense, to guidance and advice from a *soi-disant* expert about her hair. The hair is in
      'poor condition'. It is probably 'damaged'. By what? By perm lotions, neutralisers,
15   colouring agents and other of the favourite witches' brew of chemicals which are the
      hairdresser's stock-in-trade. Not to mention the plethora of gels, mousses, conditioners,

protein rinses and so on – all, of course, at extra cost. Hair driers, rollers, heated tongs don't do the hair much good either.

20 The effrontery of the hypocrisy is astonishing. As you sit and listen to all this sanctimonious tripe you are probably watching in the mirror another customer as she voluntarily offers her head for some sort of chemical bath or worse. Not a shred of reluctance or reservation about 'damage' from the practitioner at this stage. It provides self-perpetuating employment for her colleagues in the future, I suppose.

25 What hair actually <u>needs</u> for normal healthy maintenance is periodic washing with a minimum amount of shampoo, maybe a smear of conditioner and then to be allowed to dry naturally. And you don't need to be any kind of expert, self-styled or otherwise to know that.

30 The trouble is, if everyone took the common sense line, there'd be thousands of redundant hair dressers and product and equipment manufacturers. It's big business. And what about those who dignify their profession with a quasi-scientific title such as 'trichology' and write learned advice in women's magazines?

After thirty years of submission to the conning abuses of 'good' hairdressers, especially the sort who congregate in city centres and never charge less than £25 per visit, I am now shot of their less than benign attentions.

35 I have declared unilateral independence by growing my hair long. I wash it, brush it and wear it twisted in a bun on the top of my head exactly as I did as a teenager, although it's a bit greyer these days. A minor but satisfying blow for autonomy.

(A previously unpublished magazine article by Susan Elkin, 1993)

Exercise 5.3

Read the article by Susan Elkin and answer the following questions:

1. Give another word or phrase for (a) pretentious (line 2), (b) reminiscent (line 8), (c) effrontery (line 19) and (d) autonomy (line 37).

2. Find words in the passage which mean (a) self-styled and (b) academic sounding.

3. What damages hair, in the writer's opinion?

4. Explain in your own words why the writer thinks that the hairdressing profession is hyprocritical.

5. Summarise the writer's own recommendations for healthy hair.

6. Why can the writer now do without hairdressers?

7. List all the 'value judgment' words and phrases in this passage – the ones which indicate the writer's own views.

Your turn to write

1.   The article about hairdressers is intended for adults. Write a warning leaflet for teenagers about the dangers of some form of 'beauty treatment'.

2.   Imagine you are one of the boys fanning Cleopatra. Write what you tell a friend that evening when you have finished work.

3.   Write an essay comparing Shakespeare's description of Cleopatra's barge with the source he took it from. Comment in detail on Shakespeare's words and style. (You can use some of the work you did in Exercise 5.1 to help you.)

4.   Write a poem or an imaginative prose account of something you have seen or witnessed which struck you as beautiful.

5.   Research and write a factual article about swans. Include what makes them different from other birds, their food, habitat, breeding and behaviour.

6.   'Beauty is only skin deep.' How far do you agree or disagree? Write an essay setting out your views. Use examples to support your arguments.

7.   Write about beauty in any way you wish.

Grammar and punctuation

Direct and indirect speech

If we quote exactly what someone says in, for example, a story or a newspaper article, that is **direct speech**.

For example:

> 'Hair driers, rollers, heated tongs don't do the hair much good,' says Susan Elkin.

> Susan Elkin's exact words are quoted verbatim (word for word). They therefore have to be enclosed in inverted commas and need some other punctuation mark – in this case a comma – at the end.

Compare this example from a newspaper report:

> Dr Nigel Carter, the chief executive of the British Dental Health Foundation, says that even whitening toothpastes, which are largely ineffective in lightening teeth, should not be used more than twice a day, as they tend to be abrasive, and overuse may damage the surface enamel of teeth.

The journalist who interviewed Dr Carter is summarising in her own words what he has said. This is called **indirect** or **reported** speech and needs no inverted commas. It often needs a link word such as 'that' after the speech verb – in this case 'says' – because the words spoken are not the direct object of the verb.

Sometimes verbs need to be put in a different tense too.

For example:

> Susan Elkin said 'I **do not visit** hairdressers anymore.'
> Susan Elkin said that she **did not visit** hairdressers anymore.

> Mr Harvey-Maynard said 'I **have seen** enough of this class.'
> Mr Harvey-Maynard said that he **had seen** enough of this class.

Exercise 5.4

These sentences all use direct speech. Rewrite them in indirect speech. You will need to change word order and/or add or cut out words. Make sure you punctuate them correctly. Remember indirect speech is the writer summarising in his own words what someone else has said.

1. 'I first saw *Antony and Cleopatra* at Chichester Festival Theatre in 1969,' our English teacher told us.

2. 'Mysterious, beautiful;' wrote Yeats of the swans.

3. When he was elected in 1997 Tony Blair, Prime Minister, promised 'Education education, education.'

4. The Queen often begins her speeches with the words 'My husband and I.'

5. 'Lead on!' said the explorer to his companion.

6. My grandmother said 'I have just read *Bleak House*.'

Exercise 5.5

Rewrite these sentences using direct speech. You will need inverted commas:

1. The actor told his friends that he had enjoyed playing Antony.

2. Our headmaster hopes that the new building will be finished by the beginning of next term.

3. According to Dr Carter it is dangerous to whiten your teeth too often.

4. Mum had a headache so Dad asked us to be as quiet as we could.

5. Aunty Brenda told us that she had made plans to spend Christmas in Papua New Guinea this year.

6. Jamie explained that he wanted to go to Granny's via the supermarket in order to buy her some chocolates.

Hyphens as links in phrases acting as adjectives

Writers often use hyphens as links when they want to use a whole idea or an expression as if it were a single adjective:

> whiter-than-white
> glow-in-the-dark
> over-the-counter

This is quite a creative way of using language which enables the writer to come up with new, concise ways of describing things.

Exercise 5.6

Turn the following expressions into hyphen-linked adjectives and use them in sentences of your own:

1. black as night

2. one size fits all

3. open for business

4. dry as dust

5. fed up with school

Spelling and vocabulary

Shakespeare was a **playwright**. 'Wright' is a 1000-year old word from Old English (the language spoken in England before the Norman Conquest in 1066). It means a maker. So Shakespeare was a maker of plays. No prizes for guessing, then, what **cartwrights** and **wheelwrights** did for a living.

The names of many old crafts are still alive in English today – as surnames. **Baker**, **Brewer**, **Shepherd** and **Fisher** are all very common names, for example. If you have such a name it means that at some point – probably hundreds of years ago – one of your ancestors was known in his community by the job he did and that became the family name.

It is very obvious what names like **Butcher**, **Farmer** and **Miller** mean and you can probably make your own, quite long, list of such names. But what about the less obvious ones such as **Erwin**?

Exercise 5.7

Use a general dictionary or a dictionary of names to link the following surnames with their meanings:

Erwin	**wild boar friend**
Cordwainer	trader
Wainwright	blacksmith
Cooper	candle maker
Palmer	barrel maker
Goldsmith	pilgrim home from the Holy Land
Sawyer	leather worker
Chandler	a cutter of wood
Mercer	cart maker
Chapman	jeweller
Farrier	cloth merchant

'Trichologist' (hair expert) is an example of a newly invented word coined to describe a new idea, person, thing or trend. People – especially journalists – coin new words (neologisms) all the time, often by making a new version of an older word – such as 'shopaholic' or 'chocoholic' to describe people who are addicted to shopping or chocolate in the same way as alcoholics are addicted to alcohol.

Others are based on acronyms or near acronyms such as 'nimby' which stands for '**n**ot **i**n **m**y **b**ack **y**ard', and is applied to people who don't mind new building unless it's close to their own homes. Working couples without children are sometimes called 'dinkies' ('**d**ouble **i**ncome **n**o **k**ids **y**et'.)

Some of these neologisms become established and find their way into dictionaries as part of our growing and changing language. Others disappear very quickly.

Exercise 5.8

Find out what the following neologisms mean and use them in sentences of your own:

  yuppy   technophobe   workaholic   cinephile   townscape   wordsmith

  telethon   Oxfam   Ofsted   cyberspace

Autumn is one of a small group of words in which 'm' is followed by a silent n. The n, however, IS pronounced when autumn takes a syllable in its adjectival form: autum**n**al.

Other words which behave in a similar way include:

  condemn (comdem**n**ation, condem**n**atory)
  solemn (solem**n**ity)

Exercise 5.9

Put these words into the spaces in the sentences which follow:

autumnal   solemnity   columnist   condemnation   columnar

1.   Church services usually have an atmosphere of _____

2.   Simon Heffer is a regular _____ for *The Daily Telegraph*.

3.   _____ weather is only to be expected in October.

4.   At our school's main entrance is a large _____ area.

5.   Because she lied to us all she earned the _____ of almost everyone in the class.

Exercise 5.10

Shakespeare used the word 'am**or**ous' and Yeats the word 'clam**or**ous' in the extracts above.

Look carefully at the spellings of these because the nouns they come from are '*amour*' (a French word) and 'clam**our**'. When they become adjectives they lose a 'u'.

Write the adjective which comes from these nouns. They all follow the same rule:

         vigour   humour   glamour   clamour   rancour

Now make sure you know what all these words mean.

Functions of language

Using language polemically

In the article on pages 54-5, Susan Elkin is making an argued case against the hairdressing industry. Although she knows that not everyone would agree, she expresses her views in strong language and does not acknowledge that there could be another equally valid point of view. There is nothing even- handed about this writing.

Such an article is known as a **polemic** – from the Ancient Greek word *polemos*, 'war'. The author is, in a sense, waging war against hairdressers. Someone who writes (or speaks) in this style is called a **polemicist**.

But this article was intended for a magazine so it also has to entertain. That is why Susan Elkin opens her piece with a jokey 'hook' about mushrooms to get the reader's attention and make him/her read on and why she doesn't reveal what she is talking about until the third sentence. It is also why, occasionally, she uses slightly flippant expressions like 'they have yet to call customers patients' and 'blow for autonomy'.

Most of her text is a fairly serious, angry attempt to draw the attention of readers to something they may not have thought about before. It is the sort of article which would make readers react – in agreement or disagreement. So there would probably be published letters about it in the next issue of the magazine.

Susan Elkin:

- uses everyday language ('Hair driers, rollers, heated tongs don't do the hair much good either.')
- uses less common words ('plethora', 'effrontery') when she needs to because she is assuming that her reader is adult and well educated
- directly questions the reader to involve him or her ('And what happens when you get inside these hairdressers' shops?')
- ridicules hairdressers by accusing them of behaving as if they were medical practitioners
- reminds readers that hairdressers are the descendants of servants
- ends with an anecdote about her own hair to establish herself as a real, approachable and sensible person
- uses some contracted forms of words ('don't', 'there'd') to create a conversational tone
- uses personal pronouns ('I', 'you') which give the piece directness

Exercise 5.11

Write a short polemic for a magazine – two or three paragraphs – expressing angrily your views on something about which you feel, or can pretend to feel, strongly. It could be the decision not to put speed bumps in your street, the hunting ban, the attitude of the burger industry to health or anything else you wish. Use the same techniques as Susan Elkin.

Speaking and listening

1. Work in a group. Devise an advertising campaign for a tooth whitening product. You could create posters or a script for TV or radio; or an article for newspapers, magazines, internet or some other medium – you choose.

2. Work in a group of three. One of you is a hairdresser. One agrees with Susan Elkin. The third is a radio presenter. Rehearse the 3-minute conversation you will have on the programme. Perform your work to the rest of the class.

3. Work with a partner. One of you is Enobarbus, the character in *Antony and Cleopatra* who describes Cleopatra on her barge. The other is the person he is speaking to who

must respond appropriately. Work out an updated version, taking it in turns to be
Enobarbus.

4. Imagine you are W B Yeats's narrator. You have just seen the swans again this year.
    Think about what you would say to a friend about this. Write out your thoughts in prose
    using your own words. Include how you felt as well as what you saw and heard. You
    can make it up if you want to go beyond what is in the poem. Then give your speech as
    a presentation to someone else in your class.

Have you read?

These books feature beauty or beautiful people:

Ivy by Julie Hearn (2006) OUP
The White Darkness by Geraldine McCaughrean (2005) OUP
Antony and Cleopatra by William Shakespeare (Leon Garfield's lively retelling in
    Shakespeare Stories II is useful)
Any of the many versions of the traditional story of *Beauty and the Beast*, the Arthurian
    legend of *The Loathly Damsel* and the Greek legend of *Narcissus*
Troy by Adele Geras (2000)
Sisterland by Linda Newbery (2003)
Poems by W B Yeats. Collections of Yeats's poetry are in many anthologies.
Picture of Dorian Grey by Oscar Wilde (1890)
Death in Venice by Thomas Mann (1912) *

* Recommended for very keen readers and for scholars

And if you've done all that

●   Find and read the poems 'Storm in the Black Forest' by D H Lawrence and 'Pied
    Beauty' by Gerard Manley Hopkins. If you like them use them as a starting point for a
    personal collection of poems about beauty.

●   Antony and Cleopatra were a famous pair of lovers. They were real, but many of the
    stories now told about them are probably not true. Find out who these lovers in legend
    and literature were: Tristan and Isolde, Troilus and Cressida, Dido and Aeneas, Lancelot
    and Guinevere.

●   Look at some art books containing figure paintings of previous centuries or find them
    on the internet. Look at the work of, for example, Michelangelo, Rubens, Titian,
    Gainsborough and Dante Gabriel Rossetti. Or better still visit a gallery. Then look at
    some modern magazines which have photographs of fashion models and others. In what
    ways have ideas about beauty – especially for women – changed? Why do you think this
    is? You could prepare an illustrated presentation about this for the rest of the class.

Chapter 6

Risks

The narrator of Barbara Vine's novel, **Grasshopper,** *describes a very risky hobby – really an obsession – which she and a group of friends are regularly involved in.*

1   The most difficult kinds of roof to walk on are those on buildings put up in the past 100 years. These roofs are usually tiled, either with peg tiles or pantiles, and they slope steeply. It is as if architects like Lutyens and Mackintosh and Voysey only realised in the twentieth century that it rains a lot here and steep slopes on roofs provide better
5   drainage. The best kinds are shallow and made of slates, preferably with a stone coping or low wall at the edge, designed to hide from view the fact that the roof slopes at all. The more ornamentation on a roof the better, the more gables, belvederes, single chimney stacks and mansarding, the easier it is to climb. Single detached houses are useless to the serious climber. Standing alone as they do, no matter how shallow their
10   roofs, no matter how many footholds the tops of their dormer windows, their pediments and parapet rails provide, they remain islands. The open air, the gap between them and the house next door, which may be several or many feet, is the sea which divides them from the continent. Climbers need terraces, each house joined to the one next door and preferably not divided from it at roof level by a stack that is a barrier to their progress, a
15   high wall spanning the breadth of the roof and carrying a dozen closely set chimney pots or cowls.

The experienced climber despises television aerials and dishes as aids to balance keeping. He treads fast and light-footed on tile and coping and window ledge. He understands that the first big mistake the climber makes is to dislodge a slate and set it
20   clattering down to ricochet off the coping and crash on the ground. He holds on only to that which is firm and steady, avoiding 100-year-old chimney pots, drainpipes and flimsy plaster mouldings. The best climbers are light in weight and supple.

Most roof sounds pass unheard by the householder who *knows* it's impossible anyone is walking in the sky up above her head. What she hears must be the wind, the rustling and
25   rasping of tree branches. Or a cat may be up there. She has seen a cat on these roofs. At the veterinary practice in St John's Wood they tell her that most of the cats they treat are brought in with broken legs. The cat on the roof or balcony sees a butterfly and leaps in pursuit of it into the shining void.

We were like cats but we saw no butterflies. Mostly we went on the roofs after dark. In
30   daylight you had the view, north London laid out below you, Hampstead Heath and Highgate Wood, the heights of Mill Hill, the canal coming out of its tunnels and entering Regent's Park, but by day you might be seen. Not everyone is in her car or

stares at the ground when she walks. Once or twice we were seen but nothing came of it. What would you think if you saw three people in blue jeans and dark sweaters up on 35 the roof of mansion flats? That they were workmen putting up an aerial of course, or doing repairs to the guttering.

By night the lights were strung out and spread and scattered below us. No unpolluted sky was ever so starry. But up where we were, above the lights, the darkness was like thin smoke, the clouds and clear spaces above us stained plum-coloured. When I first 40 began I carried a torch and Liv had the inevitable candle until Wim stopped her. We must learn to see in the dark, he said, as he did. He was our teacher, as it might be a ski instructor with a class of novices on the slopes.

At my school, on the last day of term, the fourth form traditionally played a game called 'round and round the room'. You had to circle the gym from the main entrance and back 45 without once touching the floor, and you did it by means of wall bars, a horse, a climbing frame and, of course, ropes. People who inadvertently tapped the floor with a toe were disqualified. The winner was the boy or girl to do it in the shortest time. I won it easily in my fourth-form year and got the prize, a tiny silver (silver plate) cat, but unfortunately you can't take A-levels in negotiating gyms. The roofs of Maida Vale 50 became my gym and a lot of other things besides. For a little while.

People would think you mad, or at least very eccentric, if you told them you climbed on roofs. Of course, you seldom do tell anyone because you know what the reaction will be. They don't understand. They want to know why. But you might as well shoot up some heroin or drink brandy or go dancing or climb mountains or do white-water 55 rafting. They like it or they thought they would like it when they began.

It takes a certain kind of person. No one who was afraid of heights would attempt it. No one unfit or unsure on their feet *should* attempt it. It takes a kind of lawlessness, an unconventional spirit. Claustrophobics are good at it. Some, a very few, are geniuses at it. Wim was, we weren't. Liv wasn't, and Jonny, though good, wasn't in Wim's class.

60   For us, it was the freedom we could find nowhere else, but once we had pushed ourselves to the limits of what we could do and experienced it to the full, we wanted it no longer.

(From *Grasshopper* by Barbara Vine, 2000)

Note: This novel is by Ruth Rendell, who writes some of her books as Barbara Vine.

Exercise 6.1

Read the extract from *Grasshopper* and answer the following questions:

1.   Which roofs are the best to walk on?
2.   Sum up in your own words the qualities a good roof climber needs.
3.   Why, according to the narrator, is it unlikely that anyone will report a roof climber for trespass? (You should be able to find two reasons.)
4.   What are (a) pantiles (line 2), (b) belevederes (line 7) and (c) mansarding (line 8)?
5.   What, according to the narrator, is the attraction of roof climbing?

The Lotos-Eaters

Odysseus and his men are lost on their way home from the Trojan war. In this extract, the Victorian poet Alfred Lord Tennyson describes them landing on a strange island inhabited by people who eat only the fruit of the lotos-plant. The story comes from Book IX of *The Odyssey* by Homer.

1   'Courage!' he said, and pointed toward the land,
     'This mounting wave will roll us shoreward soon.'
     In the afternoon they came unto a land
     In which it seemed always afternoon.
5   All round the coast the languid air did swoon,
     Breathing like one that hath a weary dream.
     Full-faced above the valley stood the moon;
     And like a downward smoke, the slender stream
     Along the cliff to fall and pause did seem.

10   A land of streams! Some, like a downward smoke,
     Slow-dropping veils of thinnest lawn, did go;
     And some thro' wavering lights and shadows broke,
     Rolling a slumberous sheet of foam below.
     They saw the gleaming river seaward flow
15   From the inner land: far off, three mountain tops,

Three silent pinnacles of aged snow,
Stood sunset-flush'd: and, dew'd with showery drops,
Up-clomb the shadowy pine above the woven copse.

The charmed sunset linger'd low adown
20   In the red West: thro' mountain clefts the dale
Was seen far inland, and the yellow down
Border'd with palm, and many a winding vale
And meadow, set with slender galingale;[1]
A land where all things always seem'd the same!
25   And round about the keel the faces pale,
Dark faces pale against the rosy flame,
The mild-eyed Lotos-eaters came.

Branches they bore of that enchanted stem,
Laden with flower and fruit, whereof they gave
30   To each, but whoso did receive of them,
And taste, to him the gushing of the wave
Far far away did seem to mourn and rave
On alien shores; and if his fellow spake,
His voice was thin, as voices from the grave;
35   And deep-asleep he seem'd, yet all awake,
And music in his ears his beating heart did make.

They sat him on the yellow sand,
Between the sun and moon upon the shore;
And sweet it was to dream of Fatherland,
40   Of child, and wife, and slave; but evermore
Most weary seem'd the sea, weary the oar,
Weary the wandering fields of barren foam.
Then someone said, 'We will return no more,'
And all at once they sang, 'Our island home
45   Is far beyond the wave; we will no longer roam.'

[1] A spice similar to ginger.

(Alfred Lord Tennyson, 1809-1892. 'The Lotos-Eaters' was first published in 1832.)

Exercise 6.2

Read the 'Lotos-Eaters' and answer the following questions:

1.   Describe the island in your own words.
2.   What did the inhabitants of the island give the sailors and what effect did it have on them?

3. Explain the meaning of (a) languid (line 5), (b) alien (line 33) and (c) barren (line 42).

4. Choose and comment on five or six words which Tennyson chooses for their sound and the atmosphere they help to create.

5. Look carefully at the way Tennyson has arranged his verses and at the rhyme pattern. What do you think this adds to the poem?

University of Oxford Statement of Health and Safety Policy

1 1. The general provisions of the Health and Safety at Work etc Act 1974 impose a duty on all employers to ensure, as far as is reasonably practicable, the safety of their employees at work by maintaining safe plant, safe systems of work, and safe premises, and also by ensuring adequate instruction, training and supervision. The
5 University is also bound by the Act to ensure the safety of all other persons, who (though not employees) may be affected by the University's work activities.

2. The University has established the Health and Safety Management Committee as a committee of Council with the responsibility to determine the health and safety management strategy and policies necessary for the University to discharge its legal
10 obligations regarding health and safety. There is also a Consultative Committee for Health and Safety, which includes representatives of the recognised trades unions together with others representing a wide spectrum of interest in the University. The Consultative Committee will advise the Health and Safety Management Committee on all new health and safety policies and is expected to determine the appropriate
15 health and safety culture for the University.

The Chairman of the Health and Safety Management Committee, who also chairs the Consultative Committee, is appointed by the Vice-Chancellor.

The Health and Safety Management Committee has appointed three specialist advisory groups to advise on radiation protection, biological safety and occupational
20 health. It has also appointed a finance sub-committee to oversee expenditure on all matters relating to the programmes of work undertaken on the grounds of safety.

3. The Act requires every employer to prepare a written statement of general policy with respect to the health and safety at work of his employees and the organisation and arrangements in force for carrying out that policy, and to bring the statement to the
25 notice of all his employees. Council therefore circulates the following Statement of Safety Policy:

It is the policy of the University, and the responsibility of Council, to adopt all reasonably practicable measures:

(a) to secure the health, safety and welfare of all employees at places of work under

30   the University's control and elsewhere when performing their duties;

(b) to protect students and other persons who are lawfully on University premises against risk to their health or safety which might arise out of activities in those places;

(c) to maintain safe plant, machinery and equipment and a safe and healthy place of work.

35   4. It is also the policy of the University to ensure that all members of the University and its staff are aware of their individual responsibility to exercise care in relation to themselves and those who work with them. To this end individuals are enjoined to:

(a) familiarise themselves with University Safety Policy and any departmental or unit safety requirements;

40   (b) take reasonable care that all procedures used are safely carried out, and seek expert advice in any case of doubt;

(c) warn of any special or newly identified hazards in existing procedures or risks in new procedures about to be introduced;

(d) report accidents or incidents promptly;

45   (e) familiarise themselves with fire and emergency drills (including the location of emergency telephones) and escape routes; and

(f) where required by University policy register with the Occupational Health Service for health surveillance purposes.

Exercise 6.3

Read the *University of Oxford Statement of Health and Safety Policy* and answer the following questions:

1.   What, in your own words, does the 1974 law insist that employers do?

2.   Who has ultimate responsibility for health and safety at the University of Oxford?

3.   Which three areas of health and safety are of particular concern to the University?

4.   Summarise what any member of staff or a student must do to safeguard his/her own health and safety and that of others.

5.   Find phrases in the passage which mean the same as (a) 'fulfilling their required role', (b) 'in order to monitor health-related issues' and (c) 'risks which have just been noticed'.

6.   What is the purpose of this document?

Your turn to write

1. Write about any experience you have of an adventurous or 'risky' activity (such as bungee jumping, parachuting, ballooning or anything else that you found exhilarating).

2. Write a story which begins **either** with someone landing on an unusual island **or** having a serious accident in a laboratory.

3. Write a poem or prose description of a place known to you which has, for some reason, a very specific atmosphere (such as Venice during carnival week, your home area on Christmas day or London in the rain, for example).

4. Imagine that you have spotted a group of young people roof-climbing. Write a letter to a newspaper expressing your views. Then write an answer from someone who disagrees with you.

5. Write an essay about Tennyson's 'The Lotos-Eaters'. Using some of the work you have already done in Exercise 6.2 as a starting point, comment on how the poet achieves his effects. Do you like the result? Explain your reasons.

6. Write about risk in any way you wish.

Grammar and punctuation

Direct and indirect questions

'Do you like Ruth Rendell's novels?' asked Mrs Garsted-Jones in our English lesson. **(direct)**

In English Mrs Garsted-Jones asked us whether (or not) we liked Ruth Rendell's novels. **(indirect)**

'Has the Health and Safety policy been circulated to all staff yet?' enquired the Vice Chancellor. **(direct)**

The Vice Chancellor wanted to know if the Health and Safety Policy had yet been circulated to all staff. **(indirect)**

The policeman's first question was about the locks on our front door. **(indirect)**

'What sort of locks do you have on your front door?' asked the policeman first. **(direct)**

Like statements (see page 56), questions can be asked directly or indirectly. The direct form needs speech marks and a question mark and tends to be shorter. It is used a lot in fiction and drama. It seems more chatty and informal.

The indirect form needs no question mark or speech marks. It often needs a conjunction like 'if' or 'whether'. It is used a lot in reports of emotions (the Vice Chancellor asked those present for their views) and in everyday conversation when you can't remember somone's exact words so you summarise or paraphrase when you retell the conversation to someone else (Mum wondered aloud why Dad was so late). In indirect questions, as in indirect statements, the tense of the verb sometimes needs to be changed (e.g. 'why **are** you singing?' – he asked why you **were** singing).

Newspaper news reports use both forms – often in the same article – for variety.

Remember that there are a number of verbs which can be used for expressing questions in your writing. They include:

> asked, questioned, wondered, enquired, queried, demanded, persisted

Exercise 6.4

Rewrite these direct questions in an indirect form. You will need to change some words. Be as creative as you wish as long as the meaning remains the same:

1. 'Can't you see I'm busy?' my brother said crossly.

2. 'Why is so little Italian taught in British schools?' questioned the Italian Ambassador during his visit to our school.

3. Mum asked: 'Have you got a minute to lay the table for supper?'

4. 'When was the battle of Waterloo?' we were asked in History today.

5. 'Are you sure it was Alexander Fleming who discovered penicillin and not Marie Curie?' Tom asked.

6. 'What's for lunch today?' wondered Ella, as she headed for the menu board.

Exercise 6.5

Rewrite these sentences to include direct questions. Each will need speech marks and a question mark:

1. Our form tutor wondered whether there was a reason for our not being in school uniform.

2. Peter's enquiry was about the train's departure time.

3. Granny was curious to know which car we had come in.

4. It was the whereabouts of Newcastle which was exciting Chloe.

5. When the school was inspected we were asked how many hours of prep we had to do.

6. The interviewer wanted to know why the member of parliament didn't vote.

Spelling and vocabulary

Adjectives which end in '-n' like 'barren' double their 'n' when they take the suffix '-ness' and become nouns. If you speak slowly both 'n' sounds are pronounced too. So:

barren (adjective) barre**n** + **n**ess = barre**nn**ess (noun)

Exercise 6.6

Convert the following adjectives to nouns and use them in sentences of your own:

keen   drunken   open   thin   even   outspoken

Archaisms

Tennyson deliberately used some words and word forms in his poem which were not used in everyday English, in 1832 and certainly aren't now. These are known as **archaisms**. He chose them because he wanted his poem to sound as if it came from a much earlier time. Tennyson's archaisms include:

up-clomb (old past tense of 'to climb' – now 'climbed')
clefts ('cuts through'. Can you think of modern words which still relate to this?)
whoso ('anyone')
spake (old past tense of verb 'to speak' – now 'spoke')

Exercise 6.7

Shakepeare's plays were first published in full in 1623, seven years after his death. The Bible was first published entirely in English in 1611. Both texts are full of archaisms.

Find out what these archaisms from The Bible and Shakespeare once meant:

brethren   divers (as an adjective)   groat   multitudes   corse   fain   hie   twain

Malapropisms

Many people misuse words because they are similar to other words in sound or spelling and so become confused. Such errors are called **malapropisms** because a very funny character named Mrs Malaprop in Richard Brinsley Sheridan's 1775 play *The Rivals* makes these mistakes all the time. For example, she says:

● 'He is the very pineapple of politeness!'

● 'She's as headstrong as an allegory on the banks of the Nile.'

She's as headstrong as an allegory on the banks of the Nile.

Exercise 6.8

Use each of these pairs of words in two separate sentences to show that you know the difference between them:

> flout, flaunt
>
> plaintiff, plaintive
>
> sceptic, septic
>
> moral, morale
>
> deprecate, depreciate

The suffix '-ee'

An employee is someone who is employed by an employer, for example, the University of Oxford. The '-ee' suffix is attached to the root verb 'employ' to create a noun which means the person is, in some sense, subjected to the action of that verb. In the same way we get:

> **devotee** (one who is devoted),
> **absentee** (one who has absented him/herself),
> **trainee** (one who is being trained)
> New '-ee' words are often made up. Some teachers call the students in their tutor group their **tutees**. When people have been vaccinated some doctors call them **vaccinees.**

Exercise 6.9

List as many examples of '-ee' words as you can.

Functions of language

Language for clarity

The University of Oxford's Health and Safety Policy has a very specific purpose. It tells people – staff, students and visitors – using the university's facilities what they have to do to stay as safe and healthy as possible and how they must behave towards others. It also has a legal function. If there is an accident the University can prove in court that it was doing everything that it should have done to prevent accidents.

The possibilities which the document is dealing with could be a matter of life and death. It is therefore written in very 'dry' formal language. It:

● contains no colourful adjectives or adverbs
● uses numbered points for clarity
● uses formal vocabulary ('determine', 'consultative')
● is fairly easy to understand and doesn't use unnecessarily complex language ('report accidents and incidents promptly')
● makes its points bluntly and in a way that can't be taken in more than one way ('to maintain safe plant, machinery and equipment and a safe and healthy place of work.')
● is not beautiful or elegant
● contains no jokes or chatty asides
● offers no opinion or anecdote
● does not avoid repetition for the sake of style.

Your school will already have a health and safety policy (as by law it must) and your teacher will be familiar with its contents. It could be useful to examine this and compare its style with the one we've studied here.

Exercise 6.10

Devise a short health and safety policy specifically for the classroom in which you have English and to apply during English lessons. Use formal language but keep it as simple as you can. Use numbered points or bullets if you wish. Write about 100-200 words.

Speaking and listening

1. Is risk an essential part of life? Discuss your views in a group of four or five. Then join another group. Share your opinions.

2. Prepare a 3-4 minute presentation about an unusual, high-risk sport, using PowerPoint if you wish and if it's available. Give your presentation to the rest of the class.

3. With your teacher's permission and help invite into school a speaker from the Royal Society for Prevention of Accidents (RoSPA). Ask him or her to talk about managing risk. Introduce your guest to the rest of the class and be prepared to ask thoughtful questions.

4. Work in a pair or a group of three. Re-read 'The Lotos-Eaters' as if you were risk assessors. Discuss all the dangers which faced the sailors. What could they have done to reduce risk?

Have you read?

These books all relate to the theme of risk, adventure and exploration in fiction or real life:

The Other Side of Truth by Beverley Naidoo (2000) Puffin
The Storm Garden by Philip Gross (2006) OUP
A Walk in the Woods by Bill Bryson (1998) Black Swan
The Kite Rider by Geraldine McCaughrean (2002) OUP
Taking on the World by Ellen McArthur (2002) Michael Joseph
Grasshopper by Barbara Vine (2000) Penguin
Race to the Pole by Ranulph Fiennes (2005) Hyperion
Into the Crocodile Nest by Benedict Allen (2005) Faber & Faber
Faber Book of Explorations edited by Benedict Allen (2004)
The Birthday Boys by Beryl Bainbridge (1996) Abacus
Seven Years in Tibet by Heinrich Harrer (1953) Flamingo *
The Small Woman by Alan Burgess (1957) Evans *

* Recommended for very keen readers and for scholars

And if you've done all that

●   Barbara Vine mentions three architects: Lutyens, Mackintosh and Voysey. Find out about them. Use books or the internet. Look at some pictures of their work. Why did they become famous and why are they still remembered?

●   Find a newspaper story (news or a feature) which uses a lot of quotations. Analyse it to see which quotes are in direct and which in indirect speech. Work out why you think the journalist has made the choices that he/she has.

●   Alfred Lord Tennyson was Queen Victoria's Poet Laureate for most of her long reign and they became good friends. Find out about Tennyson's life and home on the Isle of Wight near the Queen's holiday home and share your findings with the rest of the class.

Chapter 7

Family

Clay, the narrator of this story, lives with her parents, sister, brother and grandmother to whom she is very close. She is feeling uneasy and thinking about Gran who is away.

1   What had happened that evening wouldn't have happened if Gran had been there. I wished she'd ring but I knew she wouldn't. The last time she'd called she said that she and Beatrice were going to the beach for a few days. I pictured them sitting by their fire on the sand, next to the Pacific Ocean, under a sky full of stars, drinking wine, happily
5   smoking whatever they were smoking. I wanted to be there, not with Gran, to be Gran, to have jumped half a century, not looking forward to all the things I would be able to do but looking back on all the things I had done, without having done them.

That would be cheating. Gran said she'd earned the right to do what she liked without caring what anyone else thought. And she *had* earned it. The joke about running off to a
10   tepee in Wales, even if it was a caravan in Shropshire, wasn't really a joke. When she was at university she found she was pregnant, and her parents were very sympathetic until they found out that she and her boyfriend didn't intend to marry or even stay together. They thought she would have the baby adopted and when she refused they told her not to come home until she changed her mind, and she never did. Never changed her
15   mind and never went home again. Mum didn't know her grandparents and the man we'd always called Grandad wasn't, in fact, our grandfather. Mum was three when Gran married him. By then she had managed to get a teaching qualification and was working and everything was fine.

But the joke about the bridge players wasn't all that funny either. Mum said he'd been a
20   wonderful father to her but she often wondered if the reason he'd been happy to take her on was because he couldn't have any children of his own. He'd had mumps when he was thirteen and it had left him sterile. There was no IVF treatment or sperm donation then. As well as being an accountant he was an amateur athlete and full of energy, and they'd travelled all over the place on holidays while Mum was growing up – and then
25   he started playing bridge. Mum said it transformed him, it was almost as if he were addicted – well I suppose he was. Gran stayed with him, bored out of her skull, for five years until he died – of monomania, Gran said, but it was a heart attack. I can remember him up to the time I was about eight, being all the things Mum said he was, a wonderful grandfather the way he'd been a wonderful father, and then they went to the Isle of
30   Wight and after that I can't remember him at all. He switched himself off.

After he died Gran discovered that it hadn't just been bridge. One thing led to another, poker, casinos, he'd been gambling heavily, that was the monomania, the addiction.

He'd run up hideous debts and remortgaged the house without telling her. She was left with nothing. We didn't talk about these things, we just knew them, they were Gran's
35   back story, and Mum's; the things that had made them what they were.

(From *Turbulence* by Jan Mark, 2006)

Exercise 7.1

Read the extract from *Turbulence* and answer the following questions:

1.   What was the 'monomania' that the narrator says her step-grandfather suffered from? How and where did it start?

2.   Why did Gran quarrel with her parents?

3.   Why did Gran and her husband have no children of their own?

4.   Where did Gran have to live after she broke away from her parents?

5.   Why and how does the narrator envy her grandmother?

6.   What is Gran doing at the time of the story?

We are seven

1   A simple Child,
      That lightly draws its breath,
      And feels its life on every limb,
      What should it know of death?

5   I met a little cottage Girl:
      She was eight years old, she said;
      Her hair was thick with many a curl
      That clustered round her head.

      She had a rustic, woodland air,
10   And she was wildly clad:
      Her eyes were fair, and very fair;
      Her beauty made me glad.

      'Sisters and brothers, little Maid,
      How many may you be?'
15   'How many? Seven in all,' she said,
      And wondering looked at me.

      'And where are they? I pray you tell.'
      She answered, 'Seven are we;
      And two of us at Conway dwell,
20   And two are gone to sea.

'Two of us in the church-yard lie,
My sister and my brother;
And, in the church-yard cottage, I
Dwell near them with my mother.'

25   'You say that two at Conway dwell,
And two are gone to sea,
Yet ye are seven! I pray you tell,
Sweet Maid, how this may be.'

Then did the little Maid reply,
30   'Seven boys and girls are we;
Two of us in the church-yard lie,
Beneath the church-yard tree.'

'You run about, my little Maid,
Your limbs they are alive;
35   If two are in the church-yard laid,
Then ye are only five.'

'Their graves are green, they may be seen,'
The little Maid replied,
'Twelve steps or more from my mother's door,
40   And they are side by side.

'My stockings there I often knit,
When it is light and fair,
I take my little porringer,
And eat my supper there.

45   'The first that died was sister Jane;
In bed she moaning lay,
Till God released her of her pain;
And then she went away.

'So in the church-yard she was laid;
50   And, when the grass was dry,
Together round her grave we played,
My brother John and I.

'And when the ground was white with snow,
And I could run and slide,
55   My brother John was forced to go,
And he lies by her side.'

'How many are you, then,' said I,
'If they two are in heaven?'
Quick was the little Maid's reply,
60   'O Master! We are seven.'

'But they are dead; those two are dead!
Their spirits are in heaven!'
'Twas throwing words away; for still
The little Maid would have her will,
65   And said, 'Nay we are seven!'

(William Wordsworth, 1770-1850)

Exercise 7.2

Read the poem 'We are seven' and answer the following questions:

1.   Account, in your own words, for the seven children in the little girl's family.

2.   What does she say which interests the narrator so much?

3.   What do you notice about Wordsworth's word choices in this poem?

4.   Summarise the child's appearance in your own words.

5.   What is the real 'message' of this poem?

Clinging to the Wreckage

1   My mother's family came from Leamington Spa. I have a photograph of my grandfather
fishing; surrounded by his three daughters and a formidable wife, he's wearing a sort of
cricketing cap, a starched collar and a tweed jacket. He was, like my father's blindness,
a taboo subject and no one ever said much about him except that he was called Mr
5   Smith and his profession was, as my father said with the sole purpose of irritating my
mother, a 'bum-bailiff' or Warwickshire debt-collector. I have no idea why he shot
himself, but my mother, at the end of her life, told me that it happened while she had a
job as a schoolmistress in South Africa. She learnt of it because her family sent her out a
copy of the local paper with the announcement of her father's death carefully marked as
10   a news item which might interest her. From what she told me I understood that they sent
no covering letter.

My mother had studied art in Birmingham, to which city she bicycled daily. Later she
taught drawing in Manchester, at a Lycée in Versailles, and at a girls' school in Natal,
where she rode bareback across the veldt and swam naked under waterfalls. She was a
15   'New Woman' who read Bernard Shaw and Katherine Mansfield, whom she resembled a
little in looks. My grandmother was a High Church Anglican whose bedside table
supported a prayer-book and a crucifix, but my mother had no use at all for God,
although she was to become revered as a heroine and a saint in her middle age.

She earned these titles, of course, for putting up with my father; an almost
20   impossible task.

(John Mortimer, 1982)

Exercise 7.3

Read the extract from *Clinging to the Wreckage* and answer the following questions:

1.   What is a 'taboo subject' (line 4)?

2.   Why, do you infer, was 'putting up with my father … was an almost impossible task' for
the writer's mother?

3.   What were the circumstances in which the writer's mother learned of her father's death?

4.   What were the writer's mother's religious beliefs?

5.   Explain the meaning of the words (a) formidable (line 2) and (b) revered (line 18).

6.   Summarise in your own words the impression you have of John Mortimer's mother.

Your turn to write

1. Write about your family or a family known to you.

2. Write a short story called 'Turbulence' treating the subject in any way you wish.

3. Write a story or a poem about a family coping either with death or disability.

4. Imagine you are Clay's Gran. Write your granddaughter a letter from the Pacific coast of America.

5. Write the newspaper article which John Mortimer's mother received in South Africa.

6. Write your response to 'We are seven'. Comment on Wordsworth's choice of words, his rhyme scheme and the point of view he is exploring.

Grammar and punctuation

Placement of 'only'

Look at these sentences:

> **She only grew carrots**. (She didn't do anything else to carrots. She didn't buy them, or eat them or use them to make prints in art. All she did was to grow them.)

> **She grew only carrots** or **She grew carrots only**. (She didn't grow, for example, potatoes, runner beans or flowers. Carrots alone were what she grew.)

> **Only she grew carrots** or **She, only, grew carrots**. (Perhaps other people grew other things but she was the only grower of carrots.)

The position of the adverb 'only' changes the meaning and sometimes, as in the third example above, the punctuation changes it too.

Many speakers and writers are very careless with this, often using the first example when they mean the second.

Think carefully about what you mean and get into the habit of placing 'only' accurately.

Exercise 7.4

Write out these sentences explaining in brackets what each means:

1. Only we read 'We are seven' that morning.

2. We only read 'We are seven' that morning.

3. We read only 'We are seven' that morning.

4. We read ' We are seven' only that morning.

5. *Turbulence* is the only novel by Jan Mark that I have read.

6. *Turbulence* is the novel by Jan Mark that only I have read.

7. *Turbulence* is the novel by Jan Mark that I have only read.

Split infinitive

In English we form the infinitive or 'title' of a verb with the word 'to'. The infinitive form does not have a tense or person or stated subject. So 'to walk', 'to play', 'to sing' and so on are infinitives.

We use them all the time by hooking them onto other verbs in sentences such as 'I need **to buy** some food' or 'Shall we get ready **to swim**?'

In other languages, such as French or Latin, infinitives are usually single words: *marcher* and *ambulare* ('to walk'), *jouer* and *ludere* ('to play'), *chanter* and *canere* ('to sing').

Because in English the infinitive is a two-word structure, other words – usually adverbs – sometimes get slipped into the middle. This is the famous **split infinitive** such as 'to boldly go' or 'to happily wait'.

Some people get very excited about split infinitives and regard them as the worst grammatical mistake you can make.

On the whole they are rather inelegant and it is much better to avoid them if possible. But sometimes trying to avoid the spilt infinitive gives you such a clumsy sentence that the split is better than the alternative. It's a matter of common sense.

Exercise 7.5

Rewrite each of these sentences without the split infinitive:

1. We must be sure to carefully prepare for the exam.

2. Are you ready to quickly visit Gran?

3. Mum told us that she used to only like reading books about horses.

4. I really will try to regularly practise the trumpet.

5. Let's get ready to really enjoy ourselves.

6. Americans like to often use split infinitives.

Why do we need punctuation?

Look at these two sentences carefully:

> The policeman said, 'The accused is lying. I saw him break into the shop on Thursday night.'

> 'The policeman,' said the accused, 'is lying. I saw him break into the shop on Thursday night.'

The words are the same. But the meaning is completely changed by the punctuation.

Exercise 7.6

Make up six pairs of sentences of your own. In each pair the words should be exactly the same but punctuate them differently to change the meaning.

Spelling and vocabulary

Monomania means an obsession ('mania') with a single thing ('mono') – in the case of the narrator's step-grandfather in the extract from *Turbulence* it was gambling. Some 'mania' words are very well established:

> **megalomania** (obsession with power)
> **kleptomania** (obsessive stealing)
> **dipsomania** (obsessive drinking or alcoholism)

Journalists and others often coin new '-mania' words, neologisms, to cater for the ever-increasing range of new obsessions:

Beatlemania (obsession with the Beatles)
Euromania (obsession with wanting to be part of the European Union)
lotterymania (obsession with lotteries)

Some of these words stick and become a permanent part of the ever-changing language. Others disappear quite quickly.

Words which include the prefix 'mono-' include:

monorail (train track consisting of a singe rail)
monocle (single eye glass used instead of a pair of glasses)
monotone (a sound using only one pitch)

Exercise 7.7

Copy out these words. Write a short definition for each of them:

monologue   bibliomania   monogamy   monochrome

trichotillomania   monolingual   monosyllable   pyromania

More silent letters

In some words (those which derive from Ancient Greek) the 'h' in 'ch' is silent – as in **chemist**, **character** or **orchid** (although there are plenty of other 'ch' words in English such as 'church' and 'chimpanzee' in which the 'h' is sounded). When you are writing these silent 'h' words do not forget to put the 'h' in, for instance in **chaos** and **orchestra.**

Similarly, some words from Ancient Greek use a 'rh' in which the 'h' is silent. These include **rhubarb**, **rheumatism** and **rhinoceros**. Make sure you spell them correctly.

Exercise 7.8

Illustrate the meaning of the following words by using each in a sentence. Learn (or revise) the spelling as you work:

rhizome   charismatic   rhapsody   rhombus

chorus   chiropodist   chemotherapy   chlorine

Functions of language

Humorous language

The British sense of humour is famous all over the world. It is quirky and often involves British people healthily laughing at themselves or seeing 'the funny side' of very serious issues. Most other nationalities have difficulty understanding it.

It often depends on understatement and can be quite subtle. English humour is rarely full of 'belly laugh' jokes or 'slapstick' comedy in which, for instance, people knock each other over or throw custard pies at each other. It is often related to words and language, spoken or written. It tends to be the kind of humour which makes you grin rather than roar with laughter.

British humour often pokes fun at the British social class system (think of classic TV comedy like *Only Fools and Horses* or *To the Manor Born*). John Mortimer hints at it in his *Clinging to the Wreckage*. His father was a senior barrister and, himself, the son of a high court judge. But his mother's father was a debt-collector, unremarkably named 'Mr Smith'. So the writer's father cannot resist commenting on the difference by referring to his father-in-law as a 'bum-bailiff' 'with the sole purpose of irritating my mother'.

John Mortimer's style is a good example of the British sense of humour. He:

- uses short sentences which sometimes seem disjointed ('My mother's family came from Leamington Spa.')

- sounds serious (although he isn't)

- uses very precise, formal language to highlight how inconsequential it all is ('to which city she bicycled daily', 'whose bedside supported'). The precision of the language does not relate to the triviality of what he's describing which turns it into a joke

- mentions a lot of place names (Manchester, Versailles, Natal) – some of which, like Leamington Spa, seem faintly ridiculous

- has fun with incongruous contrasts (Leamington Spa is very English and polite compared with naked swimming in South Africa)

- doesn't dwell on the terrible time his mother must have had looking after his father, but hints at it and makes it into an understated joke. Laughing at, and making light of one's own hardships, is very British

- recalls how the only indication that his mother was given of her father's suicide was a newspaper cutting without a covering note – almost unimaginable

Exercise 7.9

Write a paragraph or two about a relation or someone you know, making it as understatedly funny as you can. Use some of the techniques which John Mortimer uses.

Speaking and listening

1.   Work in a group of four or five. Each one of you is a family member. Role play an argument.

2.   Work with a partner. Devise a short play (sketch) based on 'We are seven.'

3.   Tell a partner about a member of your family who is interesting, tiresome, entertaining, eccentric, charismatic etc. (Everyone has at least one!) Then join another pair. Each of you should describe his or her partner's relative to the rest of the group.

4.   Organise a discussion (or formal debate) on the question 'Is the traditional family disappearing and, if so, does it matter?'

5.   Present an oral book review (perhaps on one of the titles recommended in this chapter or elsewhere in this book) to a small group or to the rest of the class.

Have you read?

These books all have family as a major theme:

Turbulence by Jan Mark (2005) Hodder
Buddy by Nigel Hinton (1983) Puffin
Looking for X by Deborah Ellis (1999) Oxford
Falling Leaves by Adeline Yen Mah (1997) Penguin
Clinging to the Wreckage by John Mortimer (1982) Penguin
Brother and Sister by Joanna Trollope (2004) Black Swan
Hungry Hill by Daphne du Maurier (1943) Penguin
Germinal by Emile Zola (1885) Penguin Classics *
Ruth by Elizabeth Gaskell (1853) Penguin Classics *
What Maisie Knew by Henry James (1897) Oxford World's Classics *
Anna Karenina by Leo Tolstoy (1877) Penguin Classics *

* Recommended for very keen readers and for scholars

And if you've done all that

●   Find out about the life and work of William Wordsworth. He believed that poetry should be about the everyday lives of ordinary people like the little girl in 'We are seven' – an unusual approach in the late 18th century when he started writing.

- John Mortimer was a defence barrister. He gave up practising law to be a full-time writer of plays, TV and film scripts and books. Read at least one of his books. He is a very witty writer.

- Compulsive gambling is a recognised addiction. And, just as Alcoholics Anonymous (AA) assists people dependent on drink, there is an organisation which works with gamblers: Gamblers Anonymous. Look at *www.gamblersanonymous.co.uk*. With your teacher's help and permission, invite a speaker into school to tell you about the organisation's work and the problems faced by its members.

Chapter 8

Government

A group of farm animals has evicted the farmer and other human beings. It now runs its own farm, but there are leadership problems and it is difficult to know whom to trust and who is telling the truth. And sometimes the farm is attacked by outsiders.

1   They had won, but they were weary and bleeding. Slowly they began to limp back towards the farm. The sight of their dead comrades stretched upon the grass moved some of them to tears. And for a little while they halted in sorrowful silence at the place where the windmill had once stood. Yes, it was gone; almost the last trace of their
5   labour was gone. Even the foundations were partially destroyed. And in rebuilding it they could not this time, as before, make use of the fallen stones. This time the stones had vanished too. The force of the explosion had flung them to distances of hundreds of yards. It was as though the windmill had never been.

    As they approached the farm Squealer, who had unaccountably been absent during the
10   fighting, came skipping towards them, whisking his tale and beaming with satisfaction. And the animals heard, from the direction of the farm buildings, the solemn boom of a gun.

    'What is that gun firing for?' said Boxer.

    'To celebrate our victory!' cried Squealer.

    'What victory?' said Boxer. His knees were bleeding, he had lost a shoe and split his
15   hoof, and a dozen pellets had lodged themselves in his hindleg.

    'What victory, comrade? Have we not driven the enemy off our soil – the sacred soil of Animal Farm?'

'But they have destroyed the windmill. And we had worked on it for two years!'

20 'What matter? We will build another windmill. We will build six windmills if we feel like it. You do not appreciate, comrade, the mighty thing we have done. The enemy was in occupation of this very ground that we stand upon. And now – thanks to the leadership of Comrade Napoleon – we have won every inch of it back again!'

'Then we have won back what we had before,' said Boxer.

'That is our victory,' said Squealer.

25 They limped into the yard. The pellets under the skin of Boxer's leg smarted painfully. He saw ahead of him the painful labour of rebuilding the windmill from the foundations, and already in imagination he braced himself for the task. But for the first time it occurred to him that he was eleven years old and that perhaps his great muscles were not quite what they had been.

30 But when the animals saw the green flag flying, and heard the gun firing again – seven times it was fired in all – and heard the speech that Napoleon made, congratulating them on their conduct, it did seem to them after all that they had won a great victory. The animals slain in battle were given a solemn funeral. Boxer and Clover pulled the wagon which served as a hearse, and Napoleon himself walked at the head of the procession.

35 Two whole days were given over to celebrations. There were songs, speeches, and more firing of the gun, and a special gift of an apple was bestowed on every animal, with two ounces of corn for each bird and three biscuits for each dog. It was announced that the battle would be known as the Battle of the Windmill, and that Napoleon had created a new decoration, the Order of the Green Banner, which he had conferred upon himself.

(From *Animal Farm* by George Orwell (Eric Blair), 1945)

Exercise 8.1

Read the extract from *Animal Farm* and answer the following questions:

1. What had the animals been doing immediately before this passage opens and what is the result?

2. What is implied by 'Squealer, who had unaccountably been absent during the fighting'?

3. Who is Napoleon and what impression do you get of him from this passage?

4. What do you learn from this passage about Boxer's character?

5. Why does Squealer address the other animals as 'comrade'?

6. Think about why this passage has been included in this chapter about Government. Is this extract really about animals? Give reasons for your answer.

Henry IV part 2

In Shakespeare's play **Henry IV part 2** *it is the middle of the night, but the old king cannot sleep. He is worried about his kingdom and his son. He is also ill.*

King Henry IV:

<pre>
1   How many thousand of my poorest subjects
     Are at this hour asleep! O sleep, O gentle sleep,
     Nature's soft nurse, how have I frighted thee,
     That thou no more wilt weigh my eyelids down
5   And steep my senses in forgetfulness?
     Why rather, sleep, liest thou in smoky cribs,
     Upon uneasy pallets stretching thee
     And hushed with buzzing night-flies to thy slumber,
     Than in the perfumed chambers of the great,
10   Under the canopies of costly state,
     And lulled with sound of sweetest melody?
     O thou dull god, why liest thou with the vile
     In loathsome beds, and leavest the kingly couch
     A watch-case or a common 'larum-bell?
15   Wilt thou upon the high and giddy mast
     Seal up the ship-boy's eyes, and rock his brains
     In cradle of the rude imperious surge,
     And in the visitation of the winds,
     Who take the ruffian billows by the top,
20   Curling their monstrous heads, and hanging them
     With deafing clamour in the slippery clouds,
     That with the hurly death itself awakes?
     Canst thou, O partial sleep, give thy repose
     To the wet sea-boy in an hour so rude,
25   And in the calmest and most stillest night,
     With all the appliances and means to boot,
     Deny it to a king? Then happy low, lie down!
     Uneasy lies the head that wears a crown.
</pre>

(From *Henry IV part 2*, by William Shakespeare, 1596)

Exercise 8.2

Read the extract from *Henry IV part 2* and answer the following questions:

1. Why does King Henry envy his subjects?

2. To whom or what is most of this speech addressed?

3. List synonyms for bed(s) which Shakespeare gives Henry to use in this passage.

4. Why does he mention the ship-boy?

5. Choose two examples of alliteration, assonance and consonance (see page 121) in this speech and say why they're effective.

6. Explain in your own words what Henry means by 'Uneasy lies the head that wears a crown'.

Ugandan president re-elected

1   President Yoweri Museveni of Uganda has beaten his opponent Kizza Besigye in the first presidential elections involving more than one party in Uganda for more than 25 years.

Mr Museveni got 60% of the votes and Dr Besigye 37%. Three other candidates shared
5   the remaining 3%.

Dr Besigye is refusing to accept the result. He says that the election was unfairly conducted. But some people say that Dr Besigye lost supporters when he was accused of treason and rape last year.

European Union (EU) observers said the election arrangements were largely free and
10 fair, although in some places voters were turned away without being allowed to vote. And some boxes containing voting papers were left open so that it was possible for them to have been interfered with.

There were no reports of violence during the elections. This is very different from the 2001 local elections when there were serious outbreaks of violence.

15 As well as choosing between five presidential candidates, the 10.4 million Ugandan voters have elected 284 new members of parliament. Some members of Mr Museveni's party have lost their seats.

Mr Museveni leads the National Resistance Movement (NRM) and has been President of Uganda for 20 years. Once he was admired for leading a 'new generation of African
20 leaders'. But a lot of people are now upset because he has changed the rules so that he can put himself forward to be president again after 20 years in power. Under the old rules he would have had to step down.

But many people in Uganda were – and are – relieved to have Mr Museveni as their president because he has made life better for ordinary Ugandans. They have more
25 money and the country is pleasanter and safer to live in. For many years before Mr Museveni, Uganda was ruled first by Idi Amin and then by Milton Obote. Both these men were regarded by many as ruthless tyrants.

Once Dr Besigye was Mr Museveni's personal doctor, but the two men quarrelled when they became political rivals. It is said in Kampala, the capital of Uganda, that the pair
30   have not spoken a single word to each other for more than six years.

Although Uganda is one of the wealthier countries in Africa it relies on large amounts of money from Western countries to pay almost half of its bills.

(Slightly adapted from *www.newsademic.com*, **3 March 2006)**

Exercise 8.3

Read the article 'Ugandan president re-elected' and answer the following questions:

1.   When did Yoweri Museveni first become President of Uganda?

2.   By what percentage did Mr Museveni win the 2006 election?

3.   Explain in your own words why his opponents object to him.

4.   Explain in your own words why many people support Mr Museveni.

5.   What is Kizza Besigye's profession?

6.   What happened in 2005 which probably cost Kizza Besigye votes?

7.   How fair was the election?

Your turn to write

1.   Imagine you are a Ugandan journalist. Write an article about the re-election of Mr Museveni for your newspaper.

2.   You are a head of state (in any country or an imaginary one) who cannot sleep. Write your thoughts in prose or poetry.

3.   Boxer of *Animal Farm* is a carthorse. Write an interview with him for a magazine after the Battle of the Windmill.

4.   Write a story about a group of animals doing something original or unexpected.

5.   Write about government in any way you wish.

6.   You are one of Henry IV's servants. Write a letter home to your family about your employer's health and state of mind. Use some of what is in the passage and as much imagination as you wish.

Grammar and punctuation

Common errors

1. 'Fewer' can be used only for something which you can count, e.g. days, meals, items, books. 'Less' is used to qualify something which cannot be counted or quantified, e.g. water, colour, excitement.

    So:

    > I have **fewer than six tins** (or **less shopping**) in my supermarket trolley.

    > My car uses **less petrol** (or **fewer litres of petrol**) than yours.

2. The verb 'to lay' is transitive. So it requires an object. You can, for instance lay a table, a trail, bricks or carpets.

    So:

    > Our hens are **laying** (or have **laid**, were **laying** etc) nice, big brown eggs.

    > But the verb to lie has two meanings and is never transitive. It means (a) to tell an untruth and (b) to be in a horizontal position.

    So:

    > He **lies** all the time about his family.

    > In summer I often **lie** on a rug in the garden to read.

    But take care. The past tense of the second meaning of the verb 'to lie' confuses some people so that they muddle it with the verb 'to lay'.

    Learn:

    > Henry IV **lay** dying

    > He **had lain** sleepless for several hours.

    'Layed' does not exist. And if you don't hurry to get up on a non-school day you are, of course, having a **lie-in**, not a 'lay-in' which also doesn't exist.

3. Avoid tautology. That is using unnecessary words because they repeat something you've already said.

    For example, you never need to write or say 'return back' because 'to return' means 'to go back'. The word 'back' here would be tautologous.

    Similarly, you don't need to 'ascend up' a hill or 'shout loudly' either.

Exercise 8.4

Write out these sentences putting **fewer** or **less** into the spaces:

1. George Orwell wrote _____ books than Charles Dickens.

2. Do we need more or _____ suitcases for this year's holiday?

3. We have _____ luggage than usual.

4. Kizza Besigye got _____ votes than Yoweri Museveni in the Ugandan election.

5. This queue is for shoppers with _____ than eight items to pay for.

6. There is _____ traffic on the M25 after about eight o'clock.

7. I am trying to eat _____ .

8. That means I munch _____ chocolate bars.

Exercise 8.5

Use the verbs **to lay** or **to lie** to complete these sentences. You will need various parts of the verbs and different tenses.

1. 'Please don't _____ to me,' said the headmaster.

2. Let's _____ on the beach and rest for a while.

3. The old man had _____ on the floor for an hour before he was found.

4. Our new carpet was very well _____ .

5. 'Let us _____ these _____ to rest,' said the policeman, trying to get at the truth.

6. Black Colombian hens _____ the best eggs.

7. 'I don't enjoy a _____ in,' _____ Thomas.

8. While the twins _____ on the sofa resting, Mum _____ out their party clothes.

Exercise 8.6

Rewrite these sentences without tautology:

1. I want to re-read *Henry IV part 1* again.

2. Yoweri Museveni has been chosen as the elected president of Uganda.

3. After the Battle of the Windmill, the animals were also very tired as well.

4. In a little while I shall change my library books later.

5. All formal invitations should be replied back to.

6. Before exams it's a good idea to revise over your work.

Punctuation revision
Exercise 8.7

Punctuate these passages as a way of revising your understanding of the rules of punctuation:

1. years passed the seasons came and went the short animal lives fled by a time came when there was no one who remembered the old days before the rebellion except clover benjamin moses the raven and a number of pigs (*Animal Farm*, George Orwell)

2. the letter from guy was still on the desk where i had left it wondering why i had bothered to keep it once i had read it i tore it up and dropped the pieces in our waste bin silver watching me said are you going to am i going to what marry him this guy guy i could hardly believe it i stared at him of course im not going to marry him im too young to get married (*Grasshopper*, Barbara Vine)

3. oz is a big bloke and i am not small but it took our combined weight to shift whatever was behind the door far enough for oz to squeeze through i stayed outside and put my hand round it sandor was collapsed on the floor between the wash hand basin at one end and the lavatory at the other half sitting against the door feet against the opposite wall i couldn't see his face he didn't seem to be breathing is he dead i could only whisper it (*Turbulence*, Jan Mark)

Spelling and vocabulary

Shakespeare gives Henry IV the word **loathsome** – an adjective which describes something to be loathed.

Adjectives which have the suffix '-some', from Old English, are interesting because their stems can be nouns (**troublesome**) or verbs (**loathsome**).

There are two groups:

(a) Adjectives which describe the state suggested by the stem – for example an **adventuresome** person likes adventure.

(b) Adjectives which mean something which induce the state suggested by the stem. So a **flavoursome** food has flavours for others to enjoy and a **fearsome** person frightens others.

And some '-some' words still in use stem from words which have changed their meaning. So **cumbersome** means 'clumsy' or 'awkward' because a cumber is an old word for a burden or obstruction. Similarly **handsome** used to mean 'easy to handle'.

Journalists and others sometimes coin new '–some' words too. **Toothsome** is a fairly recent word meaning 'tasty', and **cringesome** suggests 'someone or something who/which makes you cringe'.

Exercise 8.8

Use the words below to complete the sentences:

wholesome   awesome   bothersome   irksome   tiresome   fulsome

1. Although the word ' _____ ' is often misused it really does describe accurately most people's reaction to the Pyramids.

2. Midges can be very _____ in Scotland although some people are unaffected.

3. Traffic noise is _____ when it continues all night.

4. _____ food includes fruit vegetables and home cooked dishes.

5. Mr Jones's comments about my painting were so _____ and complimentary that I didn't really believe him.

6. Boxer and the other animals on Manor Farm found the rebuilding work ____ .

Exercise 8.9

Explain the meaning of:

quarrelsome   winsome   venturesome   meddlesome   noisesome   wearisome

More silent letters

Some words in English from Ancient Greek such as **psalm, psychologist** and **pterodactyl** have a silent 'p'. In Greek the combination **ps** is one letter, **psi** (ψ). Similarly, the combination **ch** (found in words such as chorus, Christmas, technical etc.) is one letter, **chi** (χ).

Functions of Language

Satire

Animal Farm is a satirical novel. George Orwell, tongue is cheek, called it a 'fairy story'. He is using satire to make a very serious point by showing animals being taken advantage of by cleverer and more powerful animals. Their leaders – the pigs – fool them. Orwell is using his animals to show truths, as he sees them, about politics and government.

Here is another example:

If you want to get nicked, get a hat

1   I don't need to tell you what the greatest scourge of our times is. As you all know it is old ladies. The older they are the more evil and criminal they tend to be. And the really shocking ones are easily spotted, for they are inevitably to be found wearing that ultimate symbol of violence and depravity, the hat. So full marks to the Hereward pub in Ely for
5   spotting an obvious trouble-maker, 82-year-old Betty Wilbraham, when she pushed her luck, took a diabolical liberty and attempted to enter their premises wearing a titfer.

As the pub pointed out, public safety could properly be preserved only if Mrs Wilbraham removed the hat. She could then be easily identified on security cameras when she started to break bottles and smash the place up – as old ladies like her
10   inevitably tend to do. Mrs Wilbraham, rather perplexed, says that she always wears a hat and that her late mother 'wouldn't have set foot outside the house without wearing one'. So what they say about criminal dynasties is clearly true, then.

(Simon Heffer, the *Daily Telegraph*, 11 March 2006)

Simon Heffer:

- uses a 'deadpan' style pretending to believe what he says ('as you all know'), borrowing the language usually associated with criticism of youthful bad behaviour ('shocking', 'depravity', 'smash the place up', 'criminal dynasties')

- chooses exaggerated language ('a diabolical liberty')

- actually means the opposite of what he says ('so full marks')

- is fiercely critical of the Hereward pub

- sympathises with Mrs Wilbraham

- uses humour and irony to make his point ('as old ladies like her inevitably tend to do')

Exercise 8.10

Write a short piece using satire and irony to criticise, or make fun of, something or someone. Use some of the techniques Simon Heffer uses.

Speaking and listening

1. Work in a group of three. One of you is Mr Museveni, another is Dr Besigye and the third is a radio presenter. Work out your radio conversation.

2. Learn by heart the speech (soliloquy) from *Henry IV part 2*. Then work out how to speak it to make it as compelling as possible.

3. Organise a discussion or debate about the present government. What is right or wrong with it? How could it be better? Don't talk about the personalities and private lives of politicians. Try to concentrate on policies. Use newspapers and the internet as sources of information.

4. Hold a balloon debate. Five people pretend to be famous or important people from the past or the present – such as William Shakespeare, Saint Francis, Nelson Mandela, Florence Nightingale and Mrs Pankhurst. The imaginary balloon that they are all in is losing gas and dropping. The only way to save the lives of four people is to throw the fifth one out – otherwise all will die. Each 'balloonist' makes a speech explaining why he/she is too important to the world to die. Then the rest of the class votes to decide who leaves the balloon and which four stay in.

5. Tell the rest of the class about a book you have read recently, explaining why you enjoyed it and why you would recommend it.

Have you read?

These books feature various forms of government:

Animal Farm by George Orwell (1945) Penguin Modern Classics
Across the Nightingale Floor by Lian Hearn (2002) Macmillan Children's Books,
The Chocolate War by Robert Cormier (1974) Puffin Teenage Books
The Other Boleyn Girl by Philippa Gregory (2001) HarperCollins
The Dogs of War by Frederick Forsyth (1974) Arrow
Alan Clark Diaries by Alan Clark, Penguin, 1993
House of Cards by Michael Dobbs, HarperCollins, 1989
Wild Swans by Jung Chang, Flamingo, 1994 *

* Recommended for very keen readers and for scholars

And if you've done all that

- In his 1946 essay 'Politics and the English Language' George Orwell suggested these six rules for clear, concise English:

   1. Never use a metaphor, simile or other figure of speech which you are used to seeing in print.
   2. Never use a long word where a short one will do.
   3. If it is possible to cut a word out, always cut it out.
   4. Never use the passive where you can use the active.
   5. Never use a foreign phrase, a scientific word or a jargon word if you can think of an everyday English equivalent.
   6. Break any of these rules sooner than say anything outright barbarous.

   Look again at the extract from *Animal Farm* and consider how far he followed his own rules. Now look at any article from a recent newspaper. To what extent is the journalist following Orwell's rules? Would it have been a better piece of writing if he or she had followed them more closely? Can you follow these rules in your own work?

- *Henry IV part 2* is part of a sequence of 'history' plays by Shakespeare: *Richard II*, *Henry IV part 1*, *Henry IV part 2*, *Henry V*. Read some of them, see a performance or watch filmed versions. Leon Garfield's *Shakespeare Stories* (1985) retells *Richard II* and *Henry IV part 1*.

- Find out what you can about Uganda, using reference books and the internet. Make a poster for the classroom wall to share some of what you have found out with others.

Chapter 9

The front line

Stephen Wraysford is a junior officer in the first world war. He has been injured in the Battle of the Somme.

1   They emerged to find chaos. Further shelling had caused casualties in the trench and had destroyed the parapet over a length of fifty yards. They took what cover they could find. Byrne dragged Stephen's body to a relatively unscathed section while Hunt went in search of help. He was told that the regimental aid post, supposedly impregnable in its
5   dugout, had been wiped out by a direct hit.

Stephen lay on his side, with the wood of the duckboards against the skin of his face, his legs bent double by Byrne to keep him out of the way of men moving up and down. His face was covered with dirt, the pores plugged with fragments blown into them by the explosion of a German grenade. He had a piece of shrapnel in his shoulder and had
10   been hit by a rifle bullet in the neck; he was concussed by the blast and unconscious. Byrne pulled out his field dressing kit and emptied iodine into the hole in Stephen's neck; he found the tapes that pulled open the linen bag and freed the gauze dressing on its long bandage.

Rations came at ten o'clock. Byrne tried to force some rum between Stephen's lips, but
15   they would not open. In the bombardment priority was given to repairing defences and to moving the wounded who could walk. Stephen lay for a day in a niche dug for him by Byrne until a stretcher-bearer finally got him to a forward dressing station.

Stephen felt a profound weariness. He wanted to sleep in long draughts of days, twenty at a time, in perfect silence. As the consciousness returned he seemed to manage only a
20   shallow sleep. He dipped in and out of it and sometimes when he awoke he found his body had been moved. He was unaware of the pattering of rain on his face. Each time he awoke the pain seemed to have intensified.

He had the impression that time had gone into reverse and he was travelling back closer to the moment of impact. Eventually time would stop at the moment the metal pierced
25   his flesh and the pain would stay constant at that level. He yearned for sleep; with what willpower he could muster he forced away the waking world and urged himself into the darkness.

As infection set in, he began to sweat; the fever reached its height within minutes, making his body shake and his teeth rattle. His muscles were convulsed and his pulse
30   began to beat with a fierce, accelerated rhythm. The sweat soaked through his underclothes and mud-caked uniform.

By the time they had transported him to the dressing station the fever had started to recede. The pain in his arm and neck had vanished. Instead he could hear a roaring sound of blood in his ears. Sometimes it would modulate to a hum and at others rise to a
35   shriek according to how hard his heart was pumping. With the noise came a delirium. He lost touch with his physical being and believed himself to be in a house on a French boulevard in which he searched and called the name of Isabelle. With no warning he was in an English cottage, a large institution, then back in the unremembered place of his birth. He raved and shouted.

40   He could smell the harsh carbolic soap of the orphanage, then the schoolroom with its dust and chalk. He was going to die without ever having been loved, not once, not by anyone who had known him. He would die alone and unmourned. He could not forgive them – his mother or Isabelle or the man who had promised to be a father. He screamed.

'He's shouting for his mother,' said the orderly as they brought him into the tent.

45   'They always do,' said the medical officer, peeling back the field dressing Byrne had applied almost thirty hours before.

They put him out of the tent to await transport to the casualty clearing station or death, whichever should come first.

Then, under the indifferent sky his spirit left the body with its ripped flesh, infections,
50   its weak and damaged nature. While the rain fell on his arms and legs, the part of him that still lived was unreachable. It was not his mind, but some other essence that was longing now for peace on a quiet, shadowed road where no guns sounded. The deep paths of darkness opened up for it, as they opened up for other men along the lines of dug earth, barely fifty yards apart.

55   Then, as the fever in his abandoned body reached its height and he moved towards the welcome of oblivion, he heard a voice, not human, but clear and urgent. It was the sound of his life leaving him. Its tone was mocking. It offered him, instead of the peace he longed for, the possibility of return. At this late stage he could go back to his body and to the brutal perversion of life that was lived in the turned soil and torn flesh of the
60   war; he could, if he made the effort of courage and will, come back to the awkward, compromised and unconquerable existence that made up human life on earth. The voice was calling him; it appealed to his sense of shame and of curiosity unfulfilled: but if he did not heed it he would surely die.

(From *Birdsong* by Sebastian Faulks)

Exercise 9.1

1. Give other words or phrases for (a) unscathed (line 3), (b) impregnable (line 4), (c) modulate (line 34).

2. Describe Stephen's injuries.

3. How long was it before the men could get Stephen away from the fighting and what were the reasons?

4. Summarise Stephen's thoughts and ideas as he waits for treatment.

5. Do you think Stephen will die? Give detailed reasons for your answer.

Dulce et Decorum est

1 Bent double, like old beggars under sacks,
Knock-kneed, coughing like hags, we cursed through sludge,
Till on the haunting flares we turned our backs
And towards our distant rest began to trudge.
5 Men marched asleep. Many had lost their boots
But limped on, blood-shod. All went lame; all blind
Drunk with fatigue; deaf even to the hoots
Of tired, outstripped Five-Nines[1] that dropped behind.

Gas! Gas! Quick, boys – An ecstasy of fumbling,
10 Fitting the clumsy helmets just in time;
But someone still was yelling out and stumbling
And flound'ring like a man in fire or lime…
Dim, through the misty panes and thick green light,
As under a green sea, I saw him drowning.

15   In all my dreams, before my helpless sight,
      He plunges at me, guttering, choking, drowning.

      If in some smothering dreams you too could pace
      Behind the wagon we flung him in,
      His hanging face, like a devil's sick of sin;
20   If you could hear, at every jolt, the blood
      Come gargling from froth-corrupted lungs,
      Obscene as cancer, bitter as the cud
      Of vile, incurable sores on innocent tongues, –
      My friend, you would not tell with such high zest
25   To children ardent for some desperate glory,
      The old Lie: Dulce et decorum est
      Pro patria mori.[2]

(Wilfred Owen, 1893-1918)

Notes
[1] A much-hated, very destructive German high-explosive shell.
[2] A Latin tag which means 'It is sweet and right to die for your country'.

Exercise 9.2

1.   Describe in your own words what has happened to the man who is 'drowning'.

2.   Why is it difficult for the men to walk?

3.   Why does Owen call the Latin tag 'The old Lie'?

4.   Choose two of Owen's comparisons (metaphors, similes or other imagery) from the poem, comment on them and say why you think they are effective.

5.   What do the rhyme and rhythm add to the poem?

William Hillyer memoir

In this previously unpublished private family memoir, William Hillyer is writing in the 1960s at the end of his life. He recalls what he was doing in summer 1916 when he was 19 years old.

1   I left Victoria at 9am, arrived in trenches at night with a home made cake. We stayed around Loos, Hulluch, Givenchy for a little longer and then the whole division was on the move. Early June, it must have been. I remember names like Lillers, Choques, Bourg and Amiens. Our battalion stopped at Vignacourt some kilos behind Albert. For
5   some days we carried out manoeuvres capturing a village similar to the one we were to attack. All through the nights we heard convoys of guns, troops, etc. etc. going by – to the front. The big push was to begin soon. For seven nights and days there was an artillery bombardment, really terrifying. About 29th or 30th of June we moved to the

10   left of Albert into a railway cutting full of black beetles; they bothered us more than the guns.

July 1st bombardment stopped. The attack had begun. Now known as The Somme Offensive. Our division was supposed to have passed through the secondary division (quarter?) and on to the next village. The Guards were held up as we stayed in another railway cutting in company with two 12 inch guns. On the sixth of July we were moved
15   up into front trenches. We each received our mail, paid hurried visits to our friends in the different companies and then settled to our ladder to scramble out of the trenches. I had my phone, etc. etc. and a very intrepid linesman, Stuart (Staffordshire) whom I never saw often.

The next morning the attack led by our brigade soon got into difficulties. We all just
20   pushed along waiting and hoping. Then the heel of my boot chipped off and I felt a sting. I could not put my foot to the ground. I didn't know it then, but I had received a bullet which had smashed a whole mass of bones in my foot and had probably saved my life. I started to crawl back slowly, until I met the R.S.M. His duty was to stay at the back to watch for casualties or cowards.

25   Anyway I found an advanced dressing station and was injected (anti-tetanus) and attempted to . . . well I forget really. Anyway I found myself on a train. Some time later I was in hospital at Wimereux where an operation was done and a drainage tube put in.

I think that we crossed to Dover the next night. I do remember being carried through Dover Priory Station to a hospital van. Next I woke up at Rubery, near Birmingham, and
30   was put in Dudley Rd. General Hospital Birmingham. Altogether I was in and out of hospital for about a few months. For a month or 6 weeks I went to convalesce to Wootton Wawen about 5 miles from Stratford upon Avon. Another time 6 weeks at Fircroft, Bourneville's College. Cadbury's were very good. I played football on crutches here. My foot was full of diseased bone, so I had several operations to remove bits.
35   Eventually I went home on leave. I am a little confused about dates here.

I know that on Jan 6th 1917 I was sent to Shoreham Command Depot. This was a camp for B2 men to be got fit. I enjoyed myself here, met Dorothy Samways[1] and her landlady Mrs Winton. Dolly and I became extremely friendly.

Notes
[1] Dorothy ('Dolly') Samways became the writer's wife in 1921.

(An extract from the memoir of William Hillyer)

Exercise 9.3

1. Why does the writer mention so many place names?

2. What does he mean when he says that his injury probably saved his life (line 22)?

3. Why does the Regimental Sergeant Major (RSM) stay behind the front line?

4. Why did the writer and his colleague get mail and visit friends before climbing their ladders?

5. Why do you think he has forgotten some of the detail about treatment to his foot?

Your turn to write

1. Describe an occasion when you have been hurt or injured.

2. Imagine you are a young man fighting in France in 1916. Write a letter home to your sister.

3. Imagine you are Byrne in *Birdsong*. Write your diary for the day that Stephen Wraysford was injured.

4. Write an essay about 'Dulce et Decorum est.' Use some of the work you did in Exercise 9.2 to help you.

5. Write a story called 'Birdsong'.

6. Write about war in any way you wish.

Grammar and punctuation

Past participles

Past participles are adjectives formed from verbs. If one breaks a chair, for example, the chair can be described as 'broken' ('broken' is the past participle of the verb 'to break'). But they do not work on their own. Use with an auxiliary (or 'helping') verb, usually the verb 'to have', they form the perfect (as opposed to the simple past) tense. For example:

> She has **arrived**.
> We have **wondered**.
> They had **asked**.

Most past participles in English are formed by adding '-d' or '-ed' to the root verb (e.g. 'marched', 'enquired'), sometimes after removing or changing a letter such as a 'y' (e.g. 'hurried', 'worried') or doubling a letter (e.g. 'pegged', 'tinned').

But many of our commonest verbs have irregular past participles. For example:

> He has **sung**.
> My father has **spoken**.
> You have **eaten**?

Note carefully that in English the past tense of the verb uses a form which is often, but not always, identical to the past participle of the verb.

Thus:

verb	**past tense**	**past participle**
to walk	I walked	walked
to teach	I taught	taught

But note:

to swim	I swam	swum
to eat	I ate	eaten

Exercise 9.4

1. List 20 regular past participles which can follow 'I have ....'

2. List 20 irregular part participles which can follow 'He has ...'
    You can add an object if some of your verbs are transitive.

Note: In the 17th century the past participle of the verb 'to get' was 'gotten' (compare it with 'forget' and 'forgotten'). This has changed over time. In Britain we now use 'got' – e.g. 'I had just got a dog.' Early migrants to America from England in the 1600s took the language with them and it has developed differently. For example, many Americans still say 'gotten' not 'got'.

Revision

Below is some witty advice once given by a newspaper editor to his journalists because he wanted them to write clearly and well. If you have worked through all the exercises in this book (and perhaps those in *So You Really Want to Learn English Books 1 and 2* as well) you should have no difficulty working out what the editor means. His first ten rules for good writing are listed here. The other ten are included in Chapter 10.

1. Verbs has to agree with their subjects.
2. Prepositions are not words to end sentences with.
3. And don't start a sentence with a conjunction.
4. It is wrong to ever split an infinitive.
5. Avoid clichés like the plague.
6. Also, always avoid annoying alliteration.
7. Be more or less specific.
8. Parenthetical remarks (however relevant) are (usually) unnecessary.
9. No sentence fragments.
10. One should never generalise.

WARNING
Deliberate mistakes

Exercise 9.5

Take the above rules one by one and explain the point which the editor is making.

Spelling and vocabulary

The word 'perversion' means wrong or bad use. It comes from the Latin verb *per* + *vertere* meaning 'to turn the wrong way'. 'The brutal perversion' of Stephen Wraysford's life in the extract from *Birdsong* suggests that the war is treating him like an animal (or brute) by turning his life away from what is normal. To 'pervert the course of justice' is to turn it away from what is fair and right. Most often these days the words 'perversion', 'pervert' and 'perverted' are used of people whose sexual desires are turned away from what is normal.

Other words come from the Latin *vertere* with various prefixes. They include: 'invert', 'extrovert', 'advertise', 'inversion'.

Exercise 9.6

Use the following words from *vertere* in sentences to make their meaning clear:

1. diversion
2. introvert
3. vertigo
4. subvert
5. transverse
6. versus

William Hillyer describes 'manoeuvres' – or work originally done with the hands (from *manu* in Latin) but now meaning any job which is tricky and requiring special skill. 'Manipulate', 'manicure' and 'manufacture' all come from the same root. *Oeuvre* is the French word for 'work'. If we talk (in English) of the 'oeuvre' of a writer, musician, or artist, we mean everything he or she wrote, composed, made or painted – all that person's work. The Latin word for work is *opus*, and we sometimes refer to a writer's *magnum opus* as being their 'great work'.

Exercise 9.7

Put these words into the spaces in the following sentences:

manipulative   operational   manoeuvring   manicurist   opus   manufacturing

1. British industry has moved away from _____ toward saleable services.
2. Because decorated finger nails are so fashionable my hairdresser now also works as a _____ .
3. There were a lot of delays during the building but our school's new swimming pool is now _____ .

4. _____ the car round the bend into our garage takes great skill and a lot of practice.

5. Each piece of music a composer publishes is given an _____ number to distinguish it from his or her other works.

6. If you try too hard to get other people to do what you want you will be accused of being _____ .

Spelling revision

These words – or their close relatives – were discussed earlier in this book:

prophecy	conservatories	charismatic	technophobe
condemnatory	disappearance	horticulturalist	guarantor
quarrelsome	memorial		

Exercise 9.8

Revise the spellings and meanings of the words above.

Work with a partner. Take it in turns to call out the ten words above. Your partner should write down first the word correctly spelled and then its meaning. Score one mark for each spelling and one for each meaning so there is a total of 20 marks.

Make sure that you relearn carefully any that you get wrong.

Another ten words for revision are listed in Chapter 10.

Speaking and listening

1. Organise a class discussion about the rights and wrongs of war.

2. Prepare a presentation for a small group about what front line life was like in 1916. Use the information presented in this chapter. You could use also books and the internet to supplement your knowledge and for sources of extra information.

3. Learn Wilfred Owen's poem by heart and perform it for the rest of the class.

4. Work in a group of three. Take the roles of Stephen Wraysford, Wilfred Owen and William Hillyer. Discuss your experiences and express your thoughts about the war and what happened to you in it.

5. Read one of the books in the *Have you read?* section of this chapter and tell the rest of the class about it.

Functions of language

Creating poignancy

Poignancy comes from the Latin word *pungere*, 'to sting', 'pierce' or 'grieve' and suggests painful sadness. All three of the extracts in this chapter are, in their various ways, very poignant because they describe, from different points of view, the suffering in a war which killed millions of very young men, both British and German. Wilfred Owen and William Hillyer were actually there so theirs are first-hand narratives. Sebastian Faulks is looking back nearly a century and basing his story on his reading and research about the period.

Sebastian Faulks:

- describes the suffering in agonising detail
- writes in the third person but the viewpoint shifts. At first we see Stephen's injuries from Byrne's point of view. Then we're inside Stephen's head
- understates, and therefore emphasises, the horror of what's going on with the Medical Officer's comment: 'They always do.'
- varies sentence length and shape
- uses a lot of negative vocabulary ('unaware', 'unconquerable', 'unmourned', 'unremembered')

Wilfred Owen:

- uses angry, graphic images ('like old beggars', 'like a devil's sick of sin')
- spares the reader none of the horror
- openly questions the morality of war and conscription

William Hillyer:

- uses the straightforward language of an ordinary soldier at the front
- writes in hurried, often abbreviated, note form ('Bombardment stopped'. 'Now known as the Somme Offensive')
- does not use imagery
- conveys no bitterness and makes no comment about the severe pain he must surely have felt in his foot
- retains a sense of humour ('Dolly and I became extremely friendly')

Exercise 9.9

Write a paragraph of your own about men at war. Make it as poignant as you can using some of the (very varied) techniques used by Sebastian Faulks, Wilfred Owen and William Hillyer.

Have you read?

All these books feature people living though wars in different countries at different times:

In the Morning by Michael Cronin (2005) OUP
Birdsong by Sebastian Faulks (1994) Vintage
Charlotte Gray by Sebastian Faulks (1998) Vintage
A Town like Alice by Nevil Shute (1950) House of Stratus
Atonement by Ian McEwan (2001) Vintage
The Night Watch by Tracey Walters (2006) Virago
Mr Midshipman Hornblower by CS Forrester (1950) Penguin
Sharpe's Eagle by Bernard Cornwell (1981) HarperCollins
Gone with the Wind by Margaret Mitchell (1936) Pan *
Testament of Youth by Vera Britten (1933) Virago *
The Ghost Road by Pat Barker (1995) Penguin *

* Recommended for very keen readers and for scholars

And if you've done all that

- Find out about the short life of Wilfred Owen. Read some more of his poems. Then listen to *War Requiem* by Benjamin Britten. It was written for the consecration of Coventry's new cathedral in 1962 because the old one had been bombed in the Second World War. Part of *War Requiem* comprises some of Wilfred Owen's poems set to music.

- Look at the website of the Commonwealth War Graves Commission (*www.cwgc.org*). If you have basic information about them, you can often trace relations who fought or died in the 1914-18 war.

- Research the history of the Royal British Legion. It raises money each autumn by selling poppies to help victims of war and their families. But there's more to it than that.

Chapter 10

Marriage

Jane Austen set the scene for her novel Mansfield Park by describing the marriages of three sisters.

1   About thirty years ago, Miss Maria Ward of Huntingdon,
with only seven thousand pounds, had the good luck to
captivate Sir Thomas Bertram, of Mansfield Park, in the
county of Northampton, and to be raised to the rank of a
5   baronet's lady, with all the comforts and consequences of an
handsome house and large income. All Huntingdon exclaimed
on the greatness of the match, and her uncle, the lawyer, himself,
allowed her to be at least three thousand pounds short of any equitable
claim to it. She had two sisters to be benefited by her elevation; and such of their
10   acquaintance as thought Miss Ward and Miss Frances quite as handsome as Miss Maria,
did not scruple to predict their marrying with almost equal advantage. But there are not
so many men of large fortune in the world, as there are pretty women to deserve them.
Miss Ward, at the end of half a dozen years, found herself obliged to be attached to the
Rev. Mr Norris, a friend of her brother-in-law, with scarcely any private fortune, and
15   Miss Frances fared yet worse. Miss Ward's match, indeed, when it came to the point,
was not contemptible, Sir Thomas being happily able to give his friend an
income in the living of Mansfield, and Mr and Mrs Norris began their
career of conjugal felicity with very little less than a thousand a year.
But Miss Frances married, in the common phrase, to disoblige her
20   family, and by fixing on a Lieutenant of Marines, without   20
education, without fortune, or connections, did it very
thoroughly. She could hardly have made a more untoward
choice. Sir Thomas Bertram had interest, which from
25   principle as well as pride, from a general wish of doing right,
and a desire of seeing all that were connected with him in   25
situations of respectability, he would have been glad to exert
for the advantage of Lady Bertram's sister; but her husband's
profession was such as no interest could reach; and before
he had time to devise any other method of assisting them, an
30   absolute breach between the sisters had taken place. It was the   30
natural result of the conduct of each party, and such as a very
imprudent marriage almost always produces. To save herself from
useless remonstrance, Mrs Price never wrote to her family on the

subject till actually married. Lady Bertram, who was a woman of tranquil feelings, and a temper remarkably easy and indolent, 35 would have contented herself with merely giving up her sister, and thinking no more of the matter: but Mrs Norris had a spirit of activity, which could not be satisfied till she had written a long and angry letter to Fanny, to point out the folly of her conduct, and threaten her with all its possible 40 consequences. Mrs Price in her turn was injured and angry; and an answer which comprehended each sister in its bitterness, and bestowed such very disrespectful reflections upon the pride of Sir Thomas, as Mrs Norris could not possibly keep to herself, put an end to all intercourse 45 between them for a considerable period.

(From *Mansfield Park* by Jane Austen, 1814)

Exercise 10.1

1. What were the maiden (unmarried) names of (a) Lady Bertram and (b) Mrs Price?

2. What did the youngest sister do which upset her family?

3. What do you learn about Mrs Norris's character from this passage?

4. Explain in your own words the comment made by 'her uncle, the lawyer' (line 7).

5. This passage claims to be about the marriages of three couples. What is it actually about? Is there anything surprising which is not mentioned?

6. What, in the context of this passage, is meant by (a) elevation (line 9), (b) scruple (line 11), (c) remonstrance (line 33) and (d) intercourse (line 45)?

Sonnet 116

1   Let me not to the marriage of true minds
     Admit impediments; love is not love
     Which alters when it alteration finds,
     Or bends with the remover to remove.
5   O no, it is an ever fixèd mark
     That looks on tempests and is never shaken;
     It is the star to every wand'ring bark,
     Whose worth's unknown, although his height be taken.
     Love's not Time's fool, though rosy lips and cheeks

10   Within his bending sickle's compass come;
      Love alters not with his brief hours and weeks,
      But bears it out even to the edge of doom.
      If this be error and upon me proved,
15   I never writ, nor no man ever loved.

(William Shakespeare, 1609)

Exercise 10.2

1.   What does Shakespeare mean by (a) 'love is not love which alters' (lines 2-3) and (b) 'Love's not Time's fool' (line 9)?

2.   How many mentions are there of love and loving in this sonnet? What do you deduce from this?

3.   What is the sonnet's main message?

4.   How effective do you find the final rhyming couplet and what do you think it means?

5.   Shakespeare personifies Love in this sonnet. What does he tell us about the figure of Love?

Getting married this year? Better ask the bank manager first

1   Marrying could break the bank this year, with the average cost of a wedding soaring to a record £17,370.

      The five per cent national increase on last year's figure is more than twice the rate of inflation but is dwarfed by the price rise in London.

5   The cost of a wedding in the capital will be £22,906, up 13 per cent on last year.

      In the survey, published today by the insurers Weddingplan, the cost of virtually everything to do with weddings, from car hire to caterers, will increase this year.

      The survey was conducted by researchers posing as couples planning a June wedding. As always, the reception and honeymoon were by far the most expensive items.

10   Researchers approached a variety of shops, hotels and other companies to discover the costs of wedding attire, the church, flowers, transport, reception, stationery, photography as well as the rings and honeymoon.

      One glaring omission in the survey is the cost of a stag do or hen party. Increasingly, these are weekend-long events – often held abroad – that cause extensive damage to
15   bank balances and livers.

The research, which was conducted on a regional basis, shows that Northern Ireland and East Anglia will be the two least expensive places to hold a wedding this year – at least there you get a bit of change out of £16,000.

20 Outside London, Scotland appears to be the most expensive place, even if you are not Madonna.

Weddingplan has, of course, a vested interest in carrying out the survey because it wants happy couples – or their parents – to take out insurance to cover the costs if things go wrong.

'A wedding is one of the biggest financial outlays a couple will ever make,' said Mark Brown, a spokesman for the company.

25 'Given the relatively modest cost of insurance, it makes sense to protect the day and have peace of mind.

'Given that the average wedding now costs as much as a family car, it is perhaps surprising that only 15 per cent of couples take out wedding insurance to protect them should something go wrong.'

30 Since the first survey was carried out, for a June 1999 wedding, the average cost has gone up from £9,380 to this year's £17,370 – a rise of about 75 per cent in seven years.

Typical costs:

Bride's dress £683; groom and best man's suit hire £148; buying bridesmaids' dresses (one adult and one child) £303; bride's going away outfit £246.

35 Cake (three tier) £268; car hire £226; church fees £447; flowers £163; honeymoon £5,215; page boy suit hire £57; photography/video £729/595; reception £5,968; rings £1,910; stationery (invitations, orders of service, place cards) £412.

Total £17,370.

Regional costs:

40 London £22,906;
Scotland £18,227;
South-West £17,971;
West Midlands £17,899;
East Midlands £17,483;
45 North £16,945;

North-East £16,944;
North-West £16,793;
South-East £16,383;
Wales £16,293;
East Anglia £15,302;
Northern Ireland £15,296.,

(David Sapsted *Daily Telegraph*, 2nd February 2006)

Exercise 10.3

1. What was the approximate cost of a London wedding in 2005?

2. What does the journalist mean when he says that a stag or hen party affects 'bank balances and livers' (line 15)?

3. What does Weddingplan want couples and parents to do and why?

4. Which aspects of a wedding are the most expensive?

5. Do you think that weddings actually need to cost these large sums?

6. Why do you think getting married in London costs over £7,000 more than getting married in East Anglia?

7. Is this an unbiased piece of reporting or does the writer's opinion come through?

Your turn to write

1. Write a story called 'Marriage of True Minds.'

2. Write a sonnet about an emotion using Shakespeare's 'Sonnet 116' as a model. Try to use the same rhythm and rhyme scheme.

3. Write your views about expensive weddings.

4. Describe a wedding that you have attended.

5. Imagine you are Mrs Frances Price. Using the information you are given in the passage from *Mansfield Park* above – and adding to it in any way you wish – write to your sister Mrs Norris telling her about your life and what you think of her views.

6. Write on the subject of marriage in any way you wish.

Grammar and punctuation

Pluperfect tense and past participles

Past participles (see Chapter 9) are used with two forms of the past tense.

They are used with the perfect tense. For example: 'I **have** noticed'; 'they **have** eaten dinner'. The auxiliary verb is in the present tense.

The further past, or pluperfect tense, uses the past tense of the auxiliary verb and pushes the action back one stage further in time. For example: 'We **had** finished'; 'you **had** left'. The implication of this is usually that the pluperfect action happened before something else in the sentence. For example:

She **had** rung her mother before she left home. (The whole sentence is in the past tense, but she rang **before** she left and the tenses make that clear.)

I started the car after I **had** checked that there was petrol in it. (It is all in the past tense but one action takes place before the other, although in this case they are expressed in a different order.)

The past tenses of the verb 'to have' are often contracted with their pronoun subjects giving: 'we'd', 'I'd', 'they'd', 'you'd' and so on.

Exercise 10.4

Use the pluperfect and other forms of the past tense to complete these sentences. Underline each use of the pluperfect tense.

1. Once Vicky _____ she _____ .
2. Ben _____ but he _____ .
3. After we _____ we _____ .
4. Before you _____ we _____ .
5. I _____ before I _____ .
6. My grandparents _____ they _____ .

Revision

Below are the remaining points about good English written for journalists by a newspaper editor. The first ten are in Chapter 9.

11. Contractions aren't necessary and shouldn't be used.
12. Don't use no double negatives.
13. Eschew ampersands & abbrevs.
14. Eliminate commas, that are, not necessary.
15. Never use a big word when a diminutive one would suffice.
16. Kill all exclamation marks!!!
17. Use words correctly, irregardless of how others use them.
18. Use the apostrophe in it's proper place and omit it when its not needed.
19. Puns are for children not groan readers.
20. Proofread carefully to see if you any words out.

WARNING
Deliberate mistakes

Exercise 10.5

Take the above sentences one by one and explain the points that the editor is making.

Vocabulary and spelling

The 'career of conjugal felicity' mentioned by Jane Austen for Mr and Mrs Norris means 'happy married life'. She deliberately used slightly pompous vocabulary here because it's the sort of thing Mrs Norris herself would have said. And, since it was a practical marriage of convenience – because of the money rather than one based on love – it probably wouldn't have been particularly 'felicitous'. Jane Austen, as so often, is being ironic.

'Conjugal' means 'joined with'. It comes from the Latin word *conjungere* ('to unite'). 'Conjunction' and 'conjugate' come from the same root. When two stars or planets move to a position which from Earth looks as if they are touching (as in an eclipse) they are said to be 'in conjunction'. We also get words such as 'junction', 'joint' and 'disjointed' from *jungere*.

Exercise 10.6

How many different meanings can you think of for the word 'joint'? List them. Then use a dictionary to help you think of more.

Exercise 10.7

For a bit of spelling and vocabulary fun see how many words you can make from the letters of DISJOINTED. Each of your words must

(a) contain an 'e', (b) have four letters or more and (c) not need a capital letter.

David Sapsted mentions wedding 'station**ery**' which means 'paper goods' and must not be confused with 'station**ary**' which means 'standing still'. There are two ways of remembering the difference:

Station**e**ry contains an 'e' for envelope.

Stationary comes, like the words status and statue, from *sto stare steti statum* ('to stand') in Latin and the root is an 'a'.

Exercise 10.8

Find, or work out, ways of remembering the difference in spelling and meaning between these five easily confused pairs. Make a note of the meaning of each.

1. compliment   complement
2. councillor   counsellor
3. elusive   illusive
4. gorilla   guerrilla
5. alter   altar

More spelling revision
Exercise 10.9

Work on these ten words with a partner until you both know all the meanings and spellings. Like the set in Chapter 9 they – or a variant of them – have all been discussed in this book.

monologue	bewildered	mnemonic	embarrass
pseudonym	rheumatism	quarrelsome	clamorous
pneumonia	openness		

Functions of language

Language for newspaper reporting

Modern newspapers include many different sorts of articles, but news stories – factual accounts of things that have happened – are still their central purpose. David Sapsted has the job of reporting to readers of the *Daily Telegraph* that a survey has been conducted by an insurance company. It shows that weddings are now very elaborate and becoming rapidly more expensive.

Journalists writing news reports are traditionally expected to answer the questions Who? What? Why? Where? and When? at the beginning of their pieces. That is why a typical news story opening might be:

> *The Queen distributed silver Maundy coins to 80 men and 80 women – signifying her age on next Friday's birthday – at a service in Guildford, Surrey, yesterday.*

Who?	The Queen
What?	she gave Maundy money to 80 men and 80 women
Why?	she'll be 80 next Friday
Where?	in Guildford
When?	yesterday

Most journalists work to a code of practice – a set of agreed rules – which says that they must not confuse news with opinion. That is why news stories are usually on pages clearly headed 'News'. Other pages, on which journalists analyse the news and state their views, have headings such as 'Comment', 'Views' or 'Analysis'.

David Sapsted:

- has a headline which makes a mild joke to signal that this story is not too serious
- summarises the article in the first three short paragraphs. You could stop reading after paragraph three but you would not have fully understood his message
- includes a lot of statistics and figures because the topic is costs

- puts in a separate list of costs for readers who want more detail
- keeps his paragraphs short – often just one sentence
- breaks his work up with side headings, often called 'cross bars' in journalism
- includes a quote from someone at the insurance company
- makes gentle fun of people who spend such high sums on weddings ('bank balances and livers')

Exercise 10.10

Write a short news article (100-200 words) for a newspaper about anything you wish. Be as direct as you can. Summarise the news first. Use the rest of it to give more detail. Use some of the techniques demonstrated by David Sapsted.

Speaking and listening

1. If you have people in your class from different cultures, organise a session in which you tell each other about wedding customs in your families.

2. Discuss marriage in a small group. What do you think is the best age to get married and why?

3. Work in a group of four. One of you is a representative of Weddingplan trying to sell a wedding insurance policy to an engaged couple and the bride's father or mother. Act out your roles.

4. Work with a partner. Rehearse a shared reading and perform it to the rest of the class.

5. With your teacher's permission invite into school a speaker from Relate, a charity which works with couples whose relationships are in difficulties. Question the speaker about Relate's work.

6. Interview a married couple who've been together for a very long time (grandparents perhaps?) about how things have changed since they were first married. You might also quiz them about what makes a long and happy marriage.

Have you read?

These books all have marriage and ideas about it at their centre:

Tamar by Mal Peet (2005) Walker
The Photograph by Penelope Lively (2003) Penguin
Second Honeymoon by Joanna Trollope (2006) Bloomsbury
Good Wives? Mary, Fanny, Jennie and Me 1945-2001 by Margaret Forster (2001) Vintage

Small Island by Andrea Levy (2004) Headline
Marie and Pierre Curie by John E Senior (1998) Sutton
Portrait of a Marriage: Vita Sackville-West and Harold Nicholson by Nigel Nicholson (1973) Phoenix
The Way We Live Now by Anthony Trollope (1875) Penguin Classics *
Vanity Fair by William Makepeace Thackeray (1848) Penguin Popular Classics *
Mansfield Park by Jane Austen (1814) Penguin Popular Classics *

* Recommended for very keen readers and for scholars

And if you've done all that

- When a couple have been married for 25 years they can celebrate their silver wedding anniversary. The 50th wedding anniversary is called a golden wedding. Find out what the 15th, 20th, 30th, 35th, 40th and 60th wedding anniversaries are called. Why were there more golden wedding anniversary parties than usual in 1995?

- Both partners in the following marriages were famous, either because they worked together or because they each achieved something separately: Leonard and Virginia Woolf; Sidney and Beatrice Webb; Pierre and Marie Curie. Find out what they did.

- The traditional ending for a story is a wedding and a happy life 'for ever after'. Think of *Snow White*, *Cinderella*, *Jane Eyre*, *Pride and Prejudice* and many others. How realistic do you think this is? Think about, and discuss, whether a wedding is an end or a beginning.

- Read and discuss this leader column published in *The Times* on 5th January 2006. Who was/is Cupid, Lady Bracknell and Thomas, Annie and Clarabel?

1   The humble mouse has replaced Cupid's quiver. Last year, more than 3.5 million single Britons used an online dating service to find romance. Instead of directing inquiries on comparative pulchritude to the mirror on the wall, 65 per cent of all those in search of a compatible mate turn now to the screen on the desk.

5   The internet's reputation as a panderer needs some burnishing. To most people, chat rooms mean chat-up rooms. But some of today's internet chaperones are as strict at protecting the reputation of their matchmaking and the virtue of their charges – mostly female – as any Victorian matron. They begin with a catechism as searching as any of
10 Lady Bracknell's inquiries: likes, dislikes, values, beliefs, favourite films and horrible habits. No chatting is allowed unless the protocol is observed, the psychometric profile completed and often the fee – real, not virtual, cash – paid up-front. Then, with suitable caveats, the lonely questor on love's tortuous path may be vouchsafed a personalised selection of three tantalising e-mail addresses. Pictures come later, though lookist sites
15 – *beautifulpeople.com* or *gorgeousnetwork.com* – will post your portrait only if found

attractive by a panting team of superficial selectors.

An online search has huge advantages. It is quick. It is open at any time in any place (even, surreptitiously, from the office). It carries none of the hangdog associations of the mournful dating agency or the drink-sodden sleaziness of the bar. And it can refine the field as narrowly as you wish: gardeners, Catholics, redheads, Chelsea fans or even steam enthusiasts. Thomas, meet Annie or Clarabel.

20

(From *The Times*, 5th January 2006)

Literary terms

The tools of poetry

Poets use tools to create poems in the same way that a wood carver uses a chisel to shape a carving or a chef uses a whisk to beat egg white. For the poet the raw material is words and the tools are the devices he or she uses to shape the words. And just like any other sort of device, every item in the poet's tool kit has a name. Some of these have been mentioned in this book and/or in *So you really want to learn English Book 1* or *2*. They are referred to in the related answer books too.

You need to know the names of the tools and what exactly they do in order to be able to write about poetry accurately and well. So here, in summary, is a list of the main ones with examples taken from the poems used in this book.

> **Alliteration** – the repetition of the same letter at the beginning of neighbouring words. You can also use the adjective **alliterative**:
>
> > . . . downward **s**moke, the **s**lender **s**tream
> >
> > ('The Lotos-Eaters' by Alfred Lord Tennyson: see page 65)
>
> **Assonance** – the repetition of the same vowel sound (not necessarily spelt the same way) inside neighbouring words. You can also use the adjective **assonant**:
>
> > pl**u**mp, **u**npecked cherries
> >
> > and the repeated
> >
> > Come b**uy**, come b**uy**
> >
> > ('Goblin Market' by Christina Rossetti: See page 18)

Caesura – a break in a line of poetry. This was usual in Latin poetry and still exists in some English poetry. It is usually marked with two vertical lines.

> Admit impediments; (II) love is not love
>
> Which alters (II) when it alteration finds,
>
> ('Sonnet 116' by William Shakespeare: see page 111)

Consonance – the repetition of consonant sounds (but not necessarily spelled the same) inside neighbouring words:

> A**l**one and pa**l**e**l**y **l**oitering
>
> (repeated several times in 'La Belle Dame Sans Merci' by John Keats: see page 7)

Enjambement – the continuation of meaning from one line of poetry into the next so that the sentence (as it were) does not end at the end of the line:

> Then all smiles stopped together. There she stands
>
> As if alive . . .
>
> ('My Last Duchess' by Robert Browning: see page 41)

Metaphor – the comparison of one thing with another by pretending that the thing described really is what it is being compared to. Like personification or a simile (see below) a metaphor is a form of image. The adjective **metaphorical** and the adverb **metaphorically** are useful too. Metaphors are not *literally* true. The man in the example below is not actually dying in water. He has been gassed:

> I saw him drowning
>
> ('Dulce et Decorum est' by Wilfred Owen: see page 101)

Onomatopoeia – the use of words to imitate sounds. A single word, like 'sneeze' can be onomatopoeic, but poets also often put words together onomatopoeically. In the example below the repeated hissing or *sibilant* and 'z' sounds suggest the sound of the insects.

> hushed with buzzing night flies
>
> (*Henry IV part 2* by William Shakespeare: see page 89)

Personification – the giving of human qualities and abilities to non-humans. Poets often personify things as a way of describing them. It creates an image or picture in the reader's mind:

> The winds were lovesick with her
>
> (*Antony and Cleopatra* by William Shakespeare: see page 52)

Simile – a comparison of one thing with another which makes it clear that it is a comparison by using the words 'like' or 'as'. It is yet another sort of image.

sodden as the bed of an ancient lake

like hammered lead

(both from 'November' by Ted Hughes: see page 28)

Many of these devices are used over and over again in the poems we study in this book. To make sure that you have understood – and to 'fix' your learning – go back and look for examples of each device in each poem.

But remember that the important thing – once you've identified the device – is to work out what it's there for, why the poet used it and what it adds to the poem . . . and that's the real joy of poetry!